Examining Effective Teacher Leadership

Examining Effective Teacher Leadership

A Case Study Approach

Sara Ray Stoelinga
Melinda M. Mangin

foreword by
Susan Moore Johnson

Teachers College
Columbia University
New York and London

Published by Teachers College Press, 1234 Amsterdam Avenue, New York, NY 10027

Library of Congress Cataloging-in-Publication Data

Stoelinga, Sara Ray.
    Examining effective teacher leadership : a case study approach / Sara Ray Stoelinga, Melinda M. Mangin ; foreword by Susan Moore Johnson.
        p. cm.
    Includes bibliographical references and index.
    ISBN 978-0-8077-5035-3 (pbk. : alk. paper) — ISBN 978-0-8077-5036-0 (hardcover : alk. paper)   1. Teacher effectiveness.   2. Educational leadership.   I. Mangin, Melinda M. II. Title.
    LB1025.3.S753 2010
    371.1—dc22

                                                                            2009039510

ISBN: 978-0-8077-5035-3 (paperback)
ISBN: 978-0-8077-5036-0 (hardcover)

Printed on acid-free paper
Manufactured in the United States of America

17   16   15   14   13   12   11   10   8   7   6   5   4   3   2   1

For our children:

Evie, Isaac, Tavish, Xiomara and Tenzin

Contents

Foreword

Since the early 1900s, schools have been organized like egg crates. Teachers, who were assumed to know both their content and pedagogy, worked independently in contiguous, separate classrooms. This flat, compartmentalized structure in which all teachers had similar responsibility and status left little apparent need or room for teacher leaders. Over the past decade, however, that has changed as accountability policies have opened a new perspective on school organization and teachers' work.

By requiring schools to succeed in educating all students, accountability has revealed the limitations of the egg-crate school. Teachers' accomplishments and shortcomings are not self-contained within their classroom, but rather contribute to the school's overall success or failure. Students move from class to class and grade to grade, carrying with them all that they have learned or not learned. It is the sum of students' learning—not the total of teachers' efforts—that determines a school's success. Today, a school with uneven instructional quality from classroom to classroom faces the very real threat of state, local, and federal sanctions.

Recognizing this, many administrators moved quickly to increase the instructional coherence and capacity of their schools. Having first introduced course sequences and common curricula across classes and grades, they subsequently appointed expert teachers to improve the practice of their less effective colleagues. This strategy has spread rapidly in the past few years and today most schools offer formal roles for teacher leaders as instructional coaches.

As positions for teacher leaders have multiplied rapidly, it has become clear that these new roles, though promising, are controversial and problematic. Much of the difficulty is grounded in the traditions and norms of the egg-crate school organization, which treats teachers as interchangeable parts and serves to reinforce the longstanding norms of the profession—egalitarianism, seniority, and autonomy (Lortie, 1975). As a school improvement strategy, relying on teacher leaders as instructional coaches challenges each of these norms. Appointing a teacher leader signals clearly that some teachers are more skilled than others, that expertise is not directly related to years of experience, and that individual teachers do not have the license to teach whatever or however they like. However, most schools launched these new roles without recognizing the persistence of these traditional norms. They failed to prepare teacher leaders and their colleagues for changes that were intended to improve the school's performance, yet were certain to provoke resistance (Donaldson, Johnson, Kirkpatrick, Marinelli, Steeling, & Szczesiul, 2008).

The problems encountered in implementing roles for teacher leaders proved to be legion. Individuals often were chosen without a formal application process, leading their peers to question why they deserved the job. Principals frequently announced the new appointments without explaining to their staff how a teacher leader's efforts could contribute to their school's vision for improvement. Meanwhile, teacher leaders were frequently left on their own to drum up business, often finding that their offers of help elicited only cold stares or closed classroom doors. Sometimes they gained admission to a classroom only to discover that the teacher they had hoped to assist expected to leave for a break rather than watch a model lesson. Teacher leaders themselves were unprepared to guide others in changing their practice. Those who were dazzling with their own students often stumbled when they used the same approaches with their colleagues. Few who accepted these new positions understood the unique needs of adult learners or what it would take to guide others in relinquishing old practices for new. The school schedule rarely provided sufficient time for observations and conferences, and many teacher leaders were asked to assume their new responsibilities on top of a full-time teaching assignment. As a result, coaching was forced to the margins of the school day, and many teachers remained skeptical about what it might offer. Thus, the introduction of new roles for teacher leaders, which at first seemed a minor alteration in the school's operations, proved to require radical change in the school's organization.

Sara Stoelinga and Melinda Mangin were among the first to recognize both the potential and the challenges of teacher leadership. Their edited collection of essays, *Effective Teacher Leadership* (Mangin & Stoelinga, 2008), provides a solid research base for those who would design and study new roles for teachers within a differentiated school organization. In their new book, *Examining Effective Teacher Leadership*, they take the next important step to ensure that teacher leadership can succeed. With a series of engaging real-world cases, they have made the work of teacher leaders come alive. Arranged in a thoughtful sequence and supported with informative teaching notes, these cases can be used to support teacher leaders and school administrators as they confront the puzzles and address the problems of introducing new roles for teachers. By reflecting on these cases, those who must make teacher leadership work in the schools can discuss and practice the following: how to assess and explain the needs of their school or district, how to provide sufficient time and use that time well to improve teaching quality, how to diagnose others' strengths and weaknesses, how to model best practice, how to nurture growth among experienced professionals, and how to gain confidence and support for a new approach to school improvement.

The promise of teacher leadership is great, but so is the risk of failure. If this approach succeeds, it will ensure not only that all students have a fair opportunity to be well educated, but also that schools become organizations where teaching is a shared responsibility, where all teachers become learners and where the boundaries between classrooms recede. For that to happen, however, both administrators and teacher leaders must recognize and prepare for the challenge. This book provides a rich a detailed guide for their new and important work.

Susan Moore Johnson

REFERENCES

Lortie, D. C. (1975). *Schoolteacher: A sociological study.* Chicago: University of Chicago Press.

Donaldson, M. L., Johnson, S. M., Kirkpatrick, C. L., Marinell, W. H., Steeling, J. L., & Szczesiul, S. A. (2008). Angling for access, bartering for change: How second-stage teachers experience differentiated roles in schools. *Teachers College Record, 110*(5), 1088–1114.

Acknowledgments

We owe a debt of gratitude to many people whose support and assistance made this book possible.

The quality of this book was increased dramatically by the comments and suggestions we received on drafts of the materials. The cases and teaching notes were used by Melinda in a course at Michigan State University. We would like to thank the students from that course, EAD 881, for their comments, critiques, and suggestions: Christine Davis, Lauren Depestel, Aaron Dobson, Andrea Fowler-Kanoza, Jennifer Gerback, Tara Hammen, Frederick Hingst, Lisa Jacobs, Theresa King, Mollissa McIntyre, Adam Mellem, Lisa Moore, Matthew Murphy, Reuben Okari, Sarah Struzik, Christy Thelen, and James Yake. The materials were also used by Sara for district professional development in the Chicago Public Schools (CPS). We would like to thank the Office of Literacy and the Office of Math and Science in the CPS for their support in this process. We also received important feedback on the materials at our demonstration session at the 2009 American Educational Research Association meeting in San Diego. We thank the attendees of that session for their insights and ideas.

Our work has benefited significantly from the insights of those at Teachers College Press. Our editor, Brian Ellerbeck, provided us with guidance in framing our early notions of the content and the format of the book. In addition, he was always available to answer our questions and to provide suggestions throughout the writing of the materials. His kind support as we worked on this project was extremely helpful. Aureliano Vázquez, Jr., provided careful editing of our manuscript. We are grateful to them and to the many other staff members at Teachers College Press who contributed to the completion of this project.

Chrysan Gallucci (University of Washington), Cynthia Carver (Michigan State University), and Jennifer Zoltners-Sherer (University of Pittsburgh) provided extensive written feedback on the proposal, shaping our conceptualization of the project in critical ways. Thank you for helping us to improve our work.

We would also like to thank the anonymous reviewers who read our manuscript. Their insights, critiques, and questions led to important improvements in this book. Their comments resulted in a significant shift in the tone of our case studies, highlighting positive aspects of the cases and successes that may not have been emphasized otherwise. The reviewers also assisted us in identifying new fields of literature for the teaching notes. We are grateful for the care with which the reviewers considered our work.

We also extend our gratitude to Susan Moore Johnson, who took time out of her busy schedule to talk with us about our work and to write the foreword. We are deeply thankful for her generous assistance, guidance, and support.

We would also like to thank the districts and schools where we conducted the field work for our case studies. We sincerely hope that we have captured the essence of your stories in our work.

We also thank David Schalliol, who contributed the photograph for our cover. We are grateful for his willingness to share his art, and all he did to assist us.

Finally, we would like to thank our families for their ongoing support and patience in our absence and absentmindedness as we spent long evenings and countless weekends moving this project from conception to completion.

Introduction

A group of 17 students from a master's program in Educational Leadership assembled for the first session of a new course called *Instructional Teacher Leadership*. As full-time educators, the students held a variety of positions and different reasons for taking the course. Some were formal teacher leaders hoping to gain a better understanding of how to support and mentor their colleagues. A few were administrators trying to build broad-based leadership capacity in their schools. Others were classroom teachers seeking a deeper understanding of the purpose of teacher leader roles and potential influences on their work.

The class session began with introductions. Students shared information about their professional backgrounds and their reasons for participating in the course. When it was Erin's turn she stated:

> I teach first grade and I've been teaching for three years. This course is perfect for me because my principal just announced that our school is going to have teacher leaders. I don't really know what that means—he only mentioned it the last three minutes of the faculty meeting but I'll be really interested to see how it plays out.

Erin's comment reflects the increasingly common experience of teachers and administrators. Across the nation, schools are turning to formal teacher leader roles as a pathway to improved teaching and learning. Unfortunately, the increase in the number of instructional teacher leadership positions has not been matched with a commensurate level of understanding of such roles. Many educators are uncertain about the purpose of these roles, what constitutes effective role design, and how to create the conditions for successful enactment. Another student, Dana, demonstrated this reality when she explained:

> I teach fourth grade and we have teacher leaders—a literacy coach actually—and it's not going very well. Teachers don't really know how to use her. I mean, she's my friend and I feel bad for her, but she's really struggling in her new role.

Dana's comment illustrates the uncertainty that surrounds these roles. Evidence from research on instructional teacher leadership indicates that role ambiguity can cause these roles to be inefficient, ineffective, and vulnerable to the whims of education reform (Mangin & Stoelinga, 2008).

This book seeks to clarify the purpose of instructional teacher leadership, the components of effective design, and the conditions necessary for successful enactment. We present research-based cases that illustrate the lived experiences of real instructional teacher leaders from diverse settings. Moreover, we provide theoretical perspectives and empirical evidence from which to analyze and assess the cases. Using research and theory to reflect upon cases of instructional teacher leadership strengthens understandings of how to create the conditions necessary to implement and support teacher leadership. As such, this is a practical book for educational practitioners. We hope that through these cases, school administrators, teacher leaders, and teachers will be better positioned to foster the conditions necessary for effective instructional teacher leadership.

THE IMPETUS BEHIND TEACHER LEADERSHIP

Contemporary conceptualizations of teacher leadership are the outcome of two trends in education. First, efforts to professionalize teaching in the 1980s and early 1990s established teachers as an important resource for school improvement. Second, the shift toward greater educational accountability at the turn of the 21st century increased attention on instructional quality. As a result of these developments, teachers have increasingly served as a source of knowledge for improving instruction. As a result, teachers' work as instructional leaders has been formalized through the creation of specific roles.

Teacher Leadership as Professionalization

In the 1980s and early 1990s education scholars emphasized the need to professionalize teaching. Advocates of professionalization claimed that the flat career structure restricted teachers' growth and failed to capitalize on teachers' knowledge. The notion of teacher professionalization was buoyed by research on teaching practices (see the process-product literature) and school designs (see the school effectiveness literature), which reinforced the idea that teachers are a key resource for improvement. Thus, the move to professionalize teaching was born out of concern that teachers' expertise was both underutilized and necessary for school improvement to occur.

One means of professionalizing teaching was to incorporate teachers into the decision-making process. It was reasoned that teachers, who are closest to the classroom, have vital information about students' needs and how to best meet those needs. In seeking teachers' knowledge schools can more accurately target high-priority needs. As a result, many schools created shared decision-making structures that incorporated teachers. It was believed that shared decision-making involved teachers in school governance, increasing the relevance and appropriateness of administrative decisions.

In addition to involving teachers in decision-making, schools developed career ladders that were intended to provide job-enhancement opportunities for teachers (Hall & McKeen, 1989; Krupp, 1987; Little, 1990). In contrast to the traditionally flat structure of teaching, career ladders enabled teachers to earn new titles and responsibilities. As a result, schools developed formal roles such as master teacher, lead teacher, mentor teacher, and team leader (Smylie, 1997). These vertical structures for teacher advancement were thought to increase performance incentives and to produce higher levels of teacher commitment and motivation. Moreover, job enhancement structures were viewed as a way to attract high-quality candidates to the profession and retain high-performing teachers. These roles provided teachers with an opportunity to take on new responsibilities in their schools and formally contribute to school leadership.

Finally, advocates reasoned that professionalization would build teacher support for reform by increasing buy-in and ownership. Including teachers in the decision-making process, providing them with new responsibilities and opportunities for input, and formally recognizing teachers' contributions increased the likelihood that teachers would endorse and support reform efforts. Teachers, charged with the task of implementation, serve as the gatekeepers to reform. Without teacher support, instructional innovations are likely to die at the classroom door. As such, teacher professionalization was a means to improve both the design and the implementation of reform efforts.

Despite the logic underlying teacher professionalization, the intended outcomes were not entirely realized. While teachers became more involved in formal school leadership structures, their involvement focused primarily on administrative and managerial tasks. Taylor and Bogotch (1994) describe teachers as attending to the dimensions of schooling furthest from teaching and learning. Thus, teacher professionalization had the unintended consequence of redirecting teachers' energy toward managerial functions and away from matters of instruction. And in many cases, teachers described having input but lacking influence, a shortcoming that further inhibited teachers from participating in decision-making forums. Not only were teachers less focused on instruction, but the roles that were developed for teachers emphasized individual job enhancement over collective improvement.

Although efforts to professionalize teaching fell short of their intended outcomes, valuable lessons were learned. First, for improvements to occur, teachers' instructional expertise must be focused directly on teaching and learning. Second, school improvement required collective capacity-building—

that is, improving the instructional practices of all teachers. These lessons
have contributed to a new focus on broad-based efforts to improve teaching
and learning, often referred to as *professional communities* or *professional
learning communities* (Bryk, Camburn, & Louis, 1999; Bryk, Sebring, Kerbow,
Rollow, & Easton, 1998; Louis & Kruse, 1995; McLaughlin & Talbert, 2001;
Murphy, Beck, Crawford, Hodges, & McGaughy, 2001; Newmann & Wehlage, 1995). Advocates contend that teacher collaboration, marked by dialogue,
sharing, inquiry, and deprivatized practice, leads to enhanced teacher outcomes,
including collective responsibility and internal accountability.

Teacher Leadership as Instructional Improvement

In the 1990s the era of professionalization gave way to an era of accountability (Chubb & Moe, 1990; Fuhrman, 1999). Advocates of accountability-
oriented practices demanded greater attention to measuring the outcomes
of instruction. Standardized test scores were used to identify low-performing
students and as the impetus for calls to improve the quality of teaching. As
a result, teacher leadership was reconceptualized as a means to build teachers' instructional capacity.

　　This shift in the conceptualization of teacher leadership has been bol-
stered by research on effective professional development, which suggests that
high-quality learning opportunities for teachers can result in instructional
improvement (Cohen & Hill, 2001; Garet, Porter, Desimone, Birman, &
Yoon, 2001). High-quality learning is more likely to occur when teachers'
professional development is instructionally focused, school-embedded, ongoing, and supported by human and material resources (Elmore & Burney,
1999; Hawley & Valli, 1999; Richardson & Placier, 2001).

　　For many school and district administrators, formal instructional teacher
leader roles can provide one possible source of high-quality professional
development. These teacher leaders can conduct workshops and facilitate
study groups. They can support improved instructional practice through co-
planning and modeling lessons, observing teaching and providing feedback.
Teacher leaders can contribute to improved collaboration among teachers,
facilitating dialogue and reflective critique, and promoting shared practices
among peers. Teacher leaders can deepen data-driven decision-making, collecting and analyzing data. By embedding learning opportunities within the
context of the school, new instructional information is more likely to be relevant to teachers and more readily implemented.

New Instructional Teacher Leader Roles

Current conceptualizations of teacher leadership build on the increased focus
on instructional improvement and a belief that teachers have the knowledge

and expertise to assist one another in the process of building collective instructional capacity. Teachers have inherent capacity to serve as instructional leaders in their schools as they work with colleagues to plan, execute, and assess instruction and subsequent student achievement. At the same time, school administrators increasingly recognize the need for formally designated teacher leaders who are released from teaching responsibilities to facilitate and coordinate instructional improvement efforts.

Formal instructional teacher leader positions have become increasingly common (Murphy, 2005). The implementation of instructional teacher leader positions has been a core component of recent education reform initiatives. Support for these positions comes from federal initiatives including Reading First and the Math Science Partnership, private foundations such as the Small Schools Coaches Collaborative funded by the Bill and Melinda Gates Foundation, large-scale comprehensive school reform models such as America's Choice and Success for All, and professional organizations like the National Staff Development Council. As a result, formal teacher leader roles have been evident in large-scale school reform efforts, as seen in New York, San Diego, Boston, and Chicago (see Datnow & Castellano, 2001; Elmore & Burney, 1999; Hightower, Knapp, Marsh, & McLaughlin, 2002; Stein, 1998; Stoelinga, 2006).

FRAMING INSTRUCTIONAL TEACHER LEADERSHIP: RESEARCH AND THEORY

The emergence of new instructional teacher leader roles implies the need for continued research on the design, effectiveness, and conditions that influence these roles. In addition, the lessons learned from research need to be incorporated into the practice of instructional teacher leadership. In this section, we frame our work as bridging research and practice. First, we discuss research on instructional teacher leadership and define the types of roles examined in this book and the theory of action behind them. Then we describe how practitioners can use this book to bridge the gap between research, theory, and practice.

The Need for Research

Instructional teacher leadership has been undertheorized and underresearched. In their analysis of scholarship on teacher leadership, York-Barr and Duke (2004) describe the existing literature as asynchronous, atheoretical, and incomplete. Since then, scholars have been working steadily to improve the quality of teacher leader research in an effort to keep pace with developments in the field (see Mangin & Stoelinga, 2008). Recent research indicates that effective teacher leaders must have deep content and procedural knowledge to mobilize collective capacity-building (Halverson & Thomas, 2008; Lord, Cress, & Miller, 2008; Manno & Firestone, 2008). Effective teacher leadership also demands careful attention to the design of the position (Mangin, 2008b) and task enactment (Mangin, 2005, 2006), goal coherence with other programs and initiatives (Camburn, Kimball, & Lowenhaupt, 2008), recognition of informal roles and school norms (Stoelinga, 2008; Supovitz, 2008), and principal support (Mangin, 2007).

Despite the growing body of research on instructional teacher leadership, most of the literature written for practitioners draws primarily on personal experience and anecdote, rather than systematic research (see Allen, 2006; Gabriel, 2005; Stone & Cuper, 2006; Sweeney, 2003; Toll, 2005). Although some of these resources are informed by content-area research, studies of teacher leadership are generally not integrated into these guides (Taylor, 2008). Moreover, much of the existing literature on teacher leadership continues to build on theories of teacher professionalization. Less attention has been paid to teacher leadership as a source of instructional improvement, the current impetus behind these roles.

The task of building a coherent body of literature that can inform instructional teacher leader role development and implementation is complicated by the confusing array of terms used to describe these positions. Titles such as *coordinator, facilitator, specialist, helper, trainer, lead, master, mentor*, and *coach* are all used to identify teacher leader roles. Moreover, use of the same title does not ensure comparable roles and responsibilities. The absence of a common vocabulary and common understandings undermines the potential of these positions and the development of a coherent body of literature that links roles, actions, and outcomes. The instructional teacher leader roles described in this book can be defined along five dimensions:

- *Formal roles.* We examine formally designated teacher leader positions with the understanding that the work of teacher leadership is intensive and requires release time from classroom teaching for effective enactment.
- *Instructionally focused.* We focus on roles that are intended to improve teachers' instructional practice.
- *Nonsupervisory.* We adhere to the notion that teacher leaders who aim to support their colleagues in instructional improvement should not serve in a supervisory or formal evaluation capacity.
- *Broad-based.* In response to the lessons of previous professionally oriented teacher leader roles, we focus on broad-based, collective capacity-building as opposed to individual job enhancement.
- *School-level.* We view teacher leadership as rooted within the school

building and teachers' classrooms. This is in contrast to district-level support roles (e.g., curriculum specialists) or professional development that takes place off-site.

In this book we focus exclusively on formal teacher leader roles, adhering to the notion that such roles should be designed and enacted to reflect relevant research. It should be noted, however, that our view on formal roles for teacher leaders does not negate the need for or existence of informal teacher leadership. We do not mean to suggest that leadership emanates exclusively from formal roles. On the contrary, the effectiveness of formal roles for teacher leaders may be dependent on broad-based leadership development of all teachers. Our purpose here is to lend greater understanding to a particular role-based conceptualization of leadership without diminishing the importance of informal or function-based conceptualizations of leadership.

We contend that the implementation of instructional teacher leader roles whose purposes are undefined jeopardizes potential gains. This harkens to an obdurate problem in the field of educational reform—the fidelity of implementation. That is, reforms that have been modified or altered cannot be expected to yield the anticipated outcomes. Education reformers commonly point to unfaithful implementation as the primary factor compromising success. On this basis, we advocate for teacher leader role design that takes into account the lessons learned from past teacher leader reforms and relevant research.

The Theory of Action

Although formal teacher leadership roles have grown increasingly common, few frameworks exist for analyzing or implementing such roles (York-Barr & Duke, 2004). Here we describe a research-based theory of action behind instructional teacher leadership. Our description is guided by a conceptual framework that outlines three key facets of formal instructional teacher leadership: the enactment of teacher leader roles, intended benefits, and conditions influencing enactment (see Figure I.1.).

In this theoretical depiction, the enactment of teacher leadership is situated within multiple contexts: the district, social relations and tensions, cultural norms, available resources, curriculum, the role design, organizational structures, and contractual factors. The teacher leader operates within these contexts as she or he interacts with the classroom teacher about issues related to instruction through the medium of professional development activities. Thus, the teacher leader serves as an instructional resource helping teachers build knowledge and skills. The content of the interaction includes instructional topics such as curriculum standards, instructional strategies,

Figure I.1. Conceptual Framework and Theory of Action

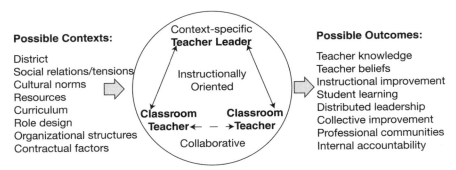

Adapted from Mangin, M. M. (2006). Teacher leadership and instructional improvement: Teachers' perspectives. In W. K. Hoy & C. Miskel (Eds.), *Contemporary issues in educational policy and school outcomes* (pp. 159–192). Greenwich, CT: Information Age Publishing.

assessment strategies, and subject matter knowledge. The process of interaction is characterized by increased dialogue, inquiry, resource-sharing, and deprivatized practice. An intermittent line between classroom teachers symbolizes teacher leadership's collaborative potential.

The possible outcomes of instructional teacher leadership include new knowledge and beliefs, instructional improvement, student learning, collective improvement, professional communities, and internal accountability. The likelihood of these outcomes depends on the extent to which the enactment of teacher leadership roles reflects research on effective instructional teacher leadership. We know that contextual factors can influence and alter the implementation of policies, programs, or theories (Berman & McLaughlin, 1977; Sabatier & Mazmanian, 1979). Moreover, this theory of instructional teacher leadership presupposes that teachers' professional development goals align with those of the district—an assumption that is not supported by research (Firestone, Mangin, Martinez, & Polovsky, 2005). Thus, teacher leaders face the challenge of balancing teachers' preferences with what we know about effective professional development.

MEETING PRACTITIONERS' NEEDS

To implement instructional teacher leader roles in accord with research and the theory of action, practitioners need more research-based resources. This book draws upon research to identify the key components of teacher leadership: *leading learning, school norms and structures, relationships, principal support,* and *data-based improvement.* In turn, these components are presented in real-life cases of elementary-level literacy and math teacher leader roles.

Case study facilitates the presentation and examination of the work that instructional teacher leaders do and the conditions in which they work. The case study method has long been recognized as a signature pedagogy in education (Bridges & Hallinger, 1995; Ivory & Gonzalez, 1999). Case study introduces readers to the experiences of real practitioners and promotes the development of problem-solving skills as the reader works to identify the key dilemmas and discern possible responses. Examining real-life cases provides readers with a deep understanding and prepares them for the challenges they will face as practitioners.

Data for the literacy-based cases were collected as part of a longitudinal research project in a large urban district undergoing educational reform. All of the literacy-based cases portray schools where 80% or more of students were eligible for free or reduced-price lunch. Data for the math-related cases studies were collected as part of a comparative study that investigated math coach roles in five small districts ranging from 2,000 to 8,000 students. Four of the five districts were among the lowest socioeconomic status districts in their state according to a ranking system that measured seven socioeconomic factors: 1) percentage of population with no high school diploma, 2) percentage with some college, 3) occupation, 4) population density, 5) income, 6) unemployment, 7) poverty. The fifth district (portrayed in Open-Ended Case 2) was a midrange district according to the socioeconomic ranking system.

Each case is accompanied by a set of teaching notes that includes learning activities, additional readings, and theoretical perspectives for analyzing the work of instructional teacher leaders. This combination of research, theory, and practice provides an opportunity for the reader to learn how to effectively design, implement, and support instructional teacher leader roles. In the sections that follow, each of the three case study formats is described in more detail.

Content and Organization

The first part of this book, "*Understanding the Work of Instructional Teacher Leaders,*" contains nine brief vignettes (approximately 800 words each) that introduce the reader to the many facets of instructional teacher leadership. The first three vignettes focus on key functions of teacher leader work. The next six vignettes describe challenges that teacher leaders face in enacting their intended roles. Each vignette provides a snapshot of varying aspects of instructional teacher leaders' work. Together, the vignettes provide an overview of the concept of instructional teacher leadership as an improvement strategy. The vignettes are accompanied by a set of teaching notes that outline learning objectives, learning activities, and suggestions for further readings. Reading the vignettes and completing the accompanying activities facilitates a thorough understanding of the functions of instructional teacher leadership and some of the barriers to effective enactment. Moreover, the reader will learn how to design teacher leader roles in ways that promote effective enactment.

The second part, "*The Dilemmas of Instructional Teacher Leadership*," uses case study to promote deep understanding of the challenges of instructional teacher leadership. This section contains five open-ended cases of medium length (aproximately 2,000 words each) that focus on five core components of teacher leadership: leading learning, school norms and structures, relationships, principal support, and data-based improvement. Each case focuses on a different core component, allowing the reader to explore in depth the dilemmas that instructional teacher leaders confront in their work. Readers will analyze the cases using research and theoretical perspectives that are central to the field of teacher leadership. Each case is accompanied by a set of teaching notes that describe the steps necessary to conduct a systematic case analysis. Analysis is guided by the question, *What* is the problem and *how* might it be addressed? By using research and theory to systematically analyze the cases, the reader will develop skills in defining, understanding, and responding to the challenges instructional teacher leaders face in their work.

The third part of the book, "*Situating Instructional Teacher Leadership in Complex Contexts*," contains three scaffolded case studies that explore instructional teacher leadership in complex school environments. The purpose of these extended cases (6,000–7,000 words each) is to consider instructional teacher leadership as it really occurs: situated in complex contexts. The scaffolded cases are structured to unfold in three sections. For instance, the Barley School case begins with a section that explores the neighborhood and school context, the second section describes the literacy initiative undertaken in the school, and the third section describes the literacy facilitator role within it. The scaffolded approach allows the reader to incrementally analyze the case as it gradually unfolds. As such, the extended case studies allow the reader to see how complex contexts, such as neighborhood, district, school culture, school governance, and instructional improvement initiative, influence instructional teacher leader role enactment. Each scaffolded case is followed by a set of teaching notes that presents a new analytical perspective, and learning activities.

Engagement with scaffolded case studies that unfold over time and within the context of complex environments will deepen student understanding of teacher leadership and the challenge of effective implementation.

In sum, the vignettes provide a snapshot of teacher leaders' work, isolating the functions teacher leaders perform and focusing on specific challenges in their work. The open-ended cases highlight five core components of teacher leaders' work, with each case focusing on one component to facilitate deep exploration of the challenges inherent in instructional teacher leadership. The scaffolded cases present teacher leader work *in situ*, integrating the functions, challenges, and components of teacher leader work and examining it within a variety of contextual influences. Collectively, the cases and activities facilitate a comprehensive understanding of the role that instructional teacher leaders can play in school improvement efforts.

Using This Book

The case studies in this volume are designed to be used in diverse settings for varied purposes. The materials can be used sequentially to create a semester-long course for undergraduate or graduate students. Alternately, individual case studies may be used for school- or district-based staff development sessions. The varied length, content, and approach of the different case studies make this volume highly adaptable. Each section and each case has been framed using research-based activities that can be used individually or cumulatively. The tables that accompany the activities have been assembled in an Appendix at the end of the book for easy reference.

While individual readers are sure to find useful information in this book, we believe that maximum benefit will be yielded by *groups* of readers. The cases and activities in this book are designed for educators to share, discuss, and construct new understandings. To facilitate dialogue and critical conversation around these cases, we have included discussion questions, activities to promote comprehension, and instructions for conducting systematic case analysis. Together these materials direct the readers to the most important aspects of teacher leadership and provide readers with the knowledge and skills necessary to analyze and interpret these roles.

While written for a variety of audiences and uses, it is important to note that our aim is not to provide "expert answers" to the challenges of teacher leadership or to present a step-by-step "how-to" book. Rather, it is a "how-to-think" book (Smylie in Mangin & Stoelinga, 2008). Our intention is to provide authentic cases about teacher leadership that compel discussion and to suggest research-based articles that can be read in conjunction with the cases so that readers develop analytical and problem-solving skills.

In sum, the purpose of this book of case studies is to provide research-based cases that can be used to facilitate greater understanding of instructional teacher leader roles and more effective implementation. To accomplish this, we present real scenarios experienced by practicing elementary-level teacher leaders, focusing on what is most important for effective teacher leadership as demonstrated by research. Next, we provide analytical perspectives from which to examine and interpret the cases, promoting readers' deep understanding of the dilemmas that instructional teacher leaders face and the possible responses to those dilemmas. And finally, the cases and materials in this book are written with practitioners in mind; all educators who hope to mobilize teachers' capacity to improve teaching and learning can benefit from this book. In particular, we hope this book will help teachers, formal teacher leaders, principals, and district-level administrators with the improvement of teacher leader roles.

Part 1

Understanding the Work of Instructional Teacher Leaders: The Vignettes

The first part of this volume contains nine short vignettes. The purpose of this section is to introduce the reader to the many facets of the instructional teacher leader's work. As such, the vignettes highlight key components of instructional teacher leadership. The vignettes prompt students to examine their understanding of teacher leadership through exploration of the following topics:

- Tasks and functions (Vignettes 1–3)
- Time management (Vignette 4)
- Relationships with teachers (Vignette 5)
- Work with other school leaders (Vignette 6)
- Work with the principal (Vignette 7)
- Influence of school norms and structures (Vignette 8)
- The teacher leader skills (Vignette 9)

Vignettes can be used as stand-alone pieces for study and interpretation. They can also be read as a collection that presents a complete picture of the instructional teacher leader role.

The Vignettes

In this vignette you will learn about Susan's work as the math specialist at Garden Side Elementary School. With the support of her principal, Susan planned a "phasing-in" of her role over 3 years. In this vignette, which focuses on the 1st year of her work, Susan used faculty presentations, demonstration lessons, and resource management as building blocks to create relationships of trust with teachers.

Beginning Steps

The library was buzzing with quiet chatter as Susan passed out the materials. Each table had a caddy with scissors, plastic tiles, crayons, and large-scale grid paper. Before Susan had a chance to introduce the activity, teachers began playing with the materials, arranging tiles on the grid paper and making patterns on the table. Susan couldn't help but feel proud of the new math culture that was growing at Garden Side, a K–5 elementary school.

At 3:15 Susan quietly raised her hand—the signal used at Garden Side to get students' attention. The teachers quieted down quickly, their eyes on Susan. As with all of the faculty meetings this year, Susan would use the first 20 minutes to share a math-related activity with the teachers.

"Today I want to talk with you about pentasquares," Susan began. "When five squares are put together so that they each share a full side with at least one other square, the resulting figure is called a pentasquare." Susan drew an example on chart paper for the teachers. "Using the grid paper or the tiles in your caddy, see how many different pentasquares you can make in five minutes." As the teachers worked, Susan surveyed the room. Everyone was busy with the materials. Some were quiet, while others feigned serious competition or gently poked fun at their math abilities.

This was Susan's 1st year as the math specialist. Before starting the position, she and her principal had designed a 3-year plan for implementing the role. This year, their goal was to build a positive math culture in the building by increasing teacher interest in math and their comfort as math learners. Susan opened each monthly faculty meeting with a hands-on math activity. The selected activities targeted areas of low student achievement

15

identified using last year's standardized test scores. Following the hands-on activity, Susan explained the mathematical concept behind the activity and its application at each grade level. Then Susan passed around a clipboard so that teachers could sign up to have Susan model a related lesson in their classroom.

After the first faculty meeting in September, only two teachers requested a model lesson: Ms. Bell in the fourth grade and Mrs. Tupper in third. However, after modeling in their classrooms the teachers passed along positive comments about the experience to grade-level colleagues, and Susan received additional requests. Each month a few more teachers were willing to open their doors to Susan. By May, Susan had modeled lessons in all but 2 of the 20 classrooms. In some classrooms she had modeled several math lessons.

Following each model lesson, Susan provided materials to the teacher as well as additional activities the teacher might use to expand the lesson. Several days later Susan stopped by the teacher's room to inquire if the teacher had used any of the materials, how the students had responded to the lessons, and if additional supports were needed. The teachers' responses varied. For example, Mr. Martin enthusiastically tried out the new materials. Ms. Small seemed to think Susan might take over all the math instruction. And Mrs. Bartlet thought the model lesson was an opportunity to leave the classroom and take a break! Susan adamantly explained to teachers that the model lessons and follow-up support were an opportunity for teachers to observe a new approach, try something they might not have done on their own, and receive support for their new learning.

To Susan, one of the biggest indicators of her success was the math study group. When the three first-grade teachers remarked on their lack of math training, Susan volunteered to run an afterschool math club for students and teachers. The club meetings provided the students with 40 minutes of supplemental math instruction once a week. The teachers either observed or participated as learners with the students. Then, after each club meeting, the teachers stayed for an additional 30 minutes to discuss the instructional strategies, the math content, and the students' progress. Even though the first-grade teachers had been supportive of the idea, Susan was relieved when they showed up to the first math club meeting and ecstatic when they stayed for the discussion afterward. Soon, two more teachers asked if they might participate. For Susan, the success of the club represented a turning point that reinforced her commitment to her role as math specialist.

Most importantly to Susan, the math club was an indicator of teachers' willingness to deepen their commitment to learning and become a community of learners. Moving forward, Susan hoped to create more opportunities for teachers to learn together. Susan had many ideas about ways to bring teachers together to work collaboratively. Ideally she wanted to work with grade-level teams or volunteer study groups to examine student work samples, create assessment rubrics, share progress on new instructional strategies, and perhaps facilitate a book study. Susan felt certain that these kinds of opportunities to engage in collaborative inquiry would have a synergistic effect. Even now, as she watched the teachers experiment with the pentasquare activity, Susan could see that they were learning from one another.

In Sum

In this vignette we see how Susan structured her work during her 1st year as the math specialist, beginning with demonstration lessons and gradually incorporating opportunities for teachers to engage in collaborative inquiry. Susan's approach reflects the findings from a 3-year study of math and science teacher leaders (Lord, Cress, & Miller, 2008). The authors explain that demonstration lessons constitute powerful learning tools that allow teacher leaders to "highlight important features of instruction" and "show the skeptics that their students [are] indeed capable of undertaking challenging work" (p. 61). The authors also note the importance of engaging in the "collegial critique or reflection" necessary to build a learning community. They explain:

> Teachers are able to accelerate and deepen their understanding of instruction when they have opportunities to observe one another teach and critically review what they see. Teacher leaders' work might have a greater strategic impact if it focused on the organization and facilitation of groups that support this goal. (Lord, Cress, & Miller, 2008, p. 73)

In this vignette, Susan understood the value of using demonstration lessons to show teachers how to incorporate new instructional strategies into their practice. She also aimed to create opportunities for teachers to interact around matters of instruction and become a community of learners.

VIGNETTE 2. TASKS AND FUNCTIONS: MATT

In this vignette, you will read about Matt, a math coordinator who worked to build teachers' math skills through weekly grade-level meetings. Matt worked with the teachers to identify students' learning needs and focus their instructional improvement efforts on those areas. By promoting collaboration in meetings and staying focused on matters of teaching and learning, Matt facilitated teachers' ability to provide high-quality math instruction.

Working with Teachers

With only 45 minutes to meet, Matt was eager to begin the grade-level meeting at Horace Mann Elementary School. He was pleased to see that all four of the third-grade teachers were present to discuss the new unit on measurement and data. Like all the Math Investigations units, this was a complex lesson with multiple steps and numerous mathematical components. Matt's goal for the meeting was to work with the teachers to set student learning benchmarks so that they could assess student progress at the next grade-level meeting. To help the teachers understand the intent of the unit, Matt wrote out a brief summary of the activity.

The students will:

1. Estimate how many paces it takes to cross the room.
2. Measure how many paces each student takes to cross the room.
3. Use accounting paper to record the number of paces it took each student to cross the room.
4. Compare the actual number of paces with their original estimation.
5. Examine the recorded measurements and look for the pace that is the "middle."
6. Learn the term *median.*
7. Engage the question, "Why are there so many different results?"
8. Learn the concept of a standard unit of measurement.
9. Measure the room using standard measurements such as inches and feet.
10. Read the book *How Big Is a Foot?*
11. Write about the measurement problem encountered in the story.

As the teachers looked over the unit summary, Matt briefly reflected upon the learning needs of the third-grade teachers. Jennifer, who was already taking notes in her grade-level composition notebook, had been working with Math Investigations for 3 years. She had a deep understanding of the student-centered philosophy behind the program and a genuine interest in learning more math content. Matt relied on Jennifer to help keep the monthly grade-level meetings instructionally focused. Each of the other three teachers had 2 years of experience with Math Investigations. Matt knew that the teachers lacked the math content knowledge necessary to feel confident teaching most Math Investigations units, although it was likely that they would be hesitant to admit it.

When the math coordinator position was created 3 years ago, there was broad consensus among the faculty that Matt was the logical person to fill the post. At that time, he was working with students as the basic skills instructor, providing supplementary math instruction. Matt was the only teacher in the building with a mathematics degree. He was also taking graduate courses in math education and working with a faculty member from a nearby university on a national grant aimed at improving math instruction. In contrast, many other teachers in the building openly expressed their dislike of math. Moreover, their instructional practice was teacher-centered, relying on rote memorization and repetitive worksheets.

Districtwide adoption of the Math Investigations program had sent the teachers at Mann Elementary into a tailspin. The new program was a radical change from their previous teaching methods. It required teachers to use inquiry-based and student-focused teaching strategies and demanded much higher levels of content knowledge than teachers had previously needed. The principal knew that teachers would need ongoing support to build their teaching skills and implement the new program. Because of the low socioeconomic status of their students, Mann Elementary was eligible for additional state funds, which the principal used to create the math coordinator position.

Matt worked with the district-level curriculum specialist to design the math coordinator role. Together they decided that Matt would meet with groups of teachers at each grade-level in weekly meetings. This way, teachers would learn how to work together and support one another in the implementation of the new math program. Moreover, they reasoned that small-group sessions would be the most efficient use of Matt's time. In addition to the grade-level meetings, Matt would work with individual teachers as necessary, providing demonstration lessons, co-planning, or meeting to talk about teachers' needs for support.

As the facilitator of the weekly grade-level meetings, Matt had three main goals. First, he aimed to strengthen teachers' math content knowledge. Second, he worked to build teachers' skills related to assessing student performance. And third, Matt promoted differentiated instruction to target students' learning needs. Most importantly, Matt strived to keep the grade-level meetings focused on teaching and learning. To do this, he worked with the teachers as they examined samples of student work, developed common assessment rubrics, and studied the content of the math units. In general, Matt found that having clear objectives, materials to examine and discuss, and time to talk all helped to keep the grade-level meetings instructionally focused.

In Sum

In this vignette, Matt used his knowledge of math to help teachers build critical skills necessary to improve their math instruction. Research on instructional teacher leadership indicates that when teacher leaders have deep content knowledge, teachers are more likely to view teacher leaders as a valuable resource and make use of their expertise (Manno & Firestone, 2008). Moreover, Matt strived to make the grade-level meetings collaborative and instructionally focused, two essential components of teacher leadership (Smylie & Marks, 2002).

VIGNETTE 3. TASKS AND FUNCTIONS: STELLA

The story of Stella illustrates the role that instructional teacher leaders play in the implementation of curricular materials. In this case, Stella was the literacy facilitator for Success for All (SFA), a comprehensive school reform model characterized by carefully scripted lessons and clearly delineated roles for teachers and support staff. Stella's role as literacy facilitator included a variety of activities, such as observing teachers, demonstration lessons, co-teaching, organizing student learning assessments, managing materials, and leading parent programs.

A Highly Defined Role

Stella Richards ran down the hallway at Ridgeland Elementary. It was 9:03 A.M. and she was 3 minutes late for the grade-level meeting for third-grade teachers. She burst into the meeting room waving a stack of papers in her hand. "I am here, I am here," she called out to the teachers as she entered the room. There was a moment of silence as the teachers turned to look at Stella. Upon taking in her disheveled appearance and sweaty brow, several teachers burst into laughter and applause. Stella bowed grandly and quickly seated herself at the table. "Let's get to it, we have a whole lot to do to improve our teaching" she told the teachers, smiling.

Stella was the Success for All literacy facilitator at Ridgeland. The school was in its 7th year using the materials, and Stella had been the literacy facilitator from the beginning. The primary components of her role focused on improving, in her mind "perfecting," the implementation of the Success for All literacy materials. To this end, Stella spent the bulk of her time visiting classrooms, co-teaching and providing teachers with feedback, leading study groups in grade-level meetings, and working with student assessment.

Stella engaged in regular observations of each of the teachers in grades K–3. She checked the lesson taught against the scope and sequence for the program. She evaluated teacher pacing within the observed class, gauging the extent to which teachers were completing activities in the number of minutes specified by the program. At times, Stella provided a demonstration lesson or co-taught lessons with teachers who were having difficulty implementing the SFA materials.

Each of the Stella's observations in classrooms was framed by pre- and post-observation conferences with the teacher. "The pre-observation reflection gives us a shared sense of the purpose and goals of the lesson," Stella explained. "The post-observation debriefing provides an opportunity for dialogue about how we can improve our teaching."

The grade-level meetings provided a forum for Stella to talk with kindergarten, first-, second-, and third-grade teachers about their implementation of the Success for All program. "We use these meetings to discuss common challenges in using the materials, to share strategies for deeper implementation, and to set goals together," Stella stated. Stella and the teachers worked together to identify a "critical challenge" to focus on in their teaching each month. They discussed the challenge in the meeting and identified two "strategies for improvement." The teachers then worked to integrate the two strategies into their instruction and reported back at the next grade-level meeting about how it worked.

Managing student assessment constituted the third major focus of Stella's role. SFA relies upon cross-grade homogeneous grouping. Every 8 weeks, teachers assess their students and groups are reorganized based on assessment results. These assessments and the resulting shifts required a great deal of Stella's time and attention. She coordinated the assessment materials and delivered them to teachers. She collected the assessments. She scored them. She reorganized the groups and assigned appropriate teachers for each group. She then redistributed teaching materials from teacher to teacher as needed. While the assessment work took a lot of time and energy, Stella viewed it as critical, both for the success of the program and for her work as an instructional teacher leader. "I think the dynamic regrouping is the most critical aspect of these materials. I believe in this philosophy of how children learn," Stella stated. "Scoring the assessments also helps me to know student strengths and weaknesses, which I can then use to help to improve teacher implementation and instruction."

A smaller portion of Stella's role was focused on outreach to parents around the SFA program, organizing SFA parent events. Each quarter, the parents of Ridgeland students were invited to a parent literacy night. The parents engaged in small cooperative learning groups using SFA materials with their children. Stella saw this as a way to get parent support and buy-in, particularly around the cross-grade homogeneous groupings, about which some parents were skeptical.

A final piece of Stella's role focused on intervention with students who need additional help and support. As a member of Ridgeland's Individual

Education Plan (IEP) team, she identified students who were struggling in the SFA program and worked with other team members to construct appropriate IEPs for those students.

Stella was generally positive about her role as an instructional teacher leader. While she found it challenging to find time for all of the components of her position, she felt that her role was well defined and integrated into the SFA program and the school.

In Sum

This vignette demonstrates the role teacher leaders play in supporting teachers' implementation of curricular materials. Research on instructional teacher leadership shows that teacher leaders are more likely to provide direct supports to teachers when they have a clear understanding of their role (Camburn, Kimball, & Lowenhaupt, 2008). In this case, Stella worked hard to enact a role that was well defined in a highly structured curriculum program.

VIGNETTE 4. TIME MANAGEMENT: MAUREEN

This vignette shares the experiences of Maureen, a math helping teacher who supported teachers in eight schools to improve their math practice. Stretched across eight schools, Maureen was faced with difficult decisions about how best to allocate her time, a challenge that was exacerbated by the design of her role.

A Balancing Act

Maureen looked at the flashing light on her telephone and sighed. She only had 45 minutes before she needed to be at School 6, a 15-minute drive away, and she wanted to eat her lunch and review her notes before running out the door. At the same time, Maureen tried to respond to teachers' messages in a timely fashion. She picked up the receiver to hear:

> Hi, Maureen, it's Nancy at School 3. I know you aren't scheduled to stop by tomorrow, but I was just looking over the lesson on angles and I'm not sure I have enough protractors. Also, since I've never done this lesson before, I'd like to ask a couple questions about it. Can you call me today during my prep period? That's 1:10 to 1:30. Talk to you then.

Without looking at her schedule, Maureen knew it would be difficult to call Nancy that afternoon. She already planned to model a multiplication lesson for a third-grade teacher. Maureen picked up the phone and dialed the number for School 3, hoping to leave a message for Nancy to call her at home that evening. Although Maureen's husband might grumble a little, she didn't mind doing schoolwork in the evening and she knew that Nancy would appreciate the help. "After all," thought Maureen to herself, "I'm supposed to be the helping teacher—I better earn my title!"

After 22 years of teaching, Maureen had welcomed a chance to get out of the classroom and apply her skills in a broader capacity as the math helping teacher. Admittedly, the first 2 years hadn't been what she had expected. The former superintendent had kept her in the central office to do administrative tasks despite the fact that the job description said she would work with teachers. Luckily, the new superintendent wanted to implement the role as originally intended—as an instructional resource for classroom teachers. In fact, the new superintendent, a former military officer, had taken a hard line on the matter. In his first month on the job he announced:

> These two helping teachers were brought out of the classroom to help other teachers. Although it would be nice to have my workload relieved, it's not a proper use of a teacher. They should be in a classroom. And I feel more than comfortable that I can do the administrative tasks. Where I really need the resources is to get the helping teachers actually helping the other teachers, not helping me.

The next week Maureen's office was relocated to the basement of an elementary school and she and her fellow helping teacher were instructed to assist teachers with the implementation of Everyday Math in all eight elementary schools. Maureen and her colleague were excited about the new duties. Together they arranged their schedules so that every week they would spend one half-day in each school and one full day planning. To maximize their time and focus their efforts, Maureen agreed to work with the teachers in the fourth through sixth grades, while her colleague focused on teachers in first through third grades. They distributed memos describing their role and the kinds of assistance they could provide. And, finally, they began to visit schools, model lessons, facilitate grade-level teams, and mentor individual teachers.

Despite Maureen's enthusiasm, it hadn't all been smooth sailing. No matter how hard she tried, it was a struggle to adequately respond to all the teachers' requests. Working in 8 different schools meant that there were almost 70 teachers to assist. And some time was wasted driving back and forth.

Having to travel also made it hard for teachers to contact her; she was almost never in her office when they called. And when they did get in touch with her, it seemed that they always needed to see her on a day when she was scheduled to be somewhere else.

Over time, teachers began to complain about Maureen's lack of availability. As their frustrations grew, they called less frequently. Maureen disliked knowing that teachers weren't getting the assistance they needed, but she didn't know what else to do—she couldn't imagine how to reduce her workload or set up a more efficient schedule. Realistically, how could she possibly provide high-quality instructional support when she had to drive all over the place? And it wasn't only the teachers who were suffering. Some days Maureen felt like a failure and wondered if she should return to the classroom.

Turning to her day planner, Maureen penciled in, "Call Nancy tonight" in case Nancy had not received the message to call her. Then, flipping to the next page, she wrote, "Set meeting with superintendent to discuss scheduling." "At least no one will say I didn't try," she thought to herself.

In Sum

This vignette highlights the dilemmas instructional teacher leaders face in determining how they will spend their time. Spread across 8 schools and 70 teachers, Maureen was confronted with long days and competing priorities. Research on instructional teacher leadership suggests that role design affects teacher leaders' work enactment (Mangin, 2008b). When teacher leaders were distributed across multiple schools, teachers had difficulty accessing the teacher leaders who often described themselves as "homeless" due to their lack of membership in any particular school community.

VIGNETTE 5. RELATIONSHIPS WITH TEACHERS: CASSIE

This vignette tells the story of Cassie, a math coordinator who supported teachers implementing Math Trailblazers. In particular, this vignette highlights Cassie's work with teachers and the challenges she faced in creating productive mentoring relationships.

Building Relationships

At 6:00 P.M. Cassie was just beginning to pack her bag to go home. She double-checked to make sure she had the Trailblazers unit on probability so that she could review the lesson that night before going to bed. Tomorrow Cassie would model the lesson in five different classrooms. Glancing at her calendar, she noted that tomorrow's schedule would be grueling. In addition to modeling the probability lessons, she needed to finalize next year's workbook orders, coordinate the collection of schoolwide recyclables, and teach the afterschool gifted and talented program. Resisting the urge to feel overwhelmed, Cassie resolutely decided to come in early the next day to get a head start. She was determined to be successful in her new role as math coordinator. It was mid-May and teachers still seemed reluctant to work with her. Despite this resistance, Cassie continued to be committed to her goal of having all teachers fully implement the new Trailblazers math program by the end of the year.

Cassie had begun her role as math coordinator in the fall. The position was created to provide support for teachers in learning constructivist approaches to teaching math as part of the new math program. Thus, Cassie shifted from being an "enrichment" teacher, working with pullout groups of students, to working with teachers in the implementation of Math Trailblazers. Although Cassie lacked experience with the Trailblazers program, she had received 4 days of training the previous summer and felt that her background as a Montessori teacher helped her understand the value of concept-based mathematics instruction. Cassie was excited to take on the new role, and she expected teachers to be eager to learn the new curriculum despite the fact that it diverged sharply from the traditional math they had taught previously. Cassie found that the work was much harder than she had anticipated, and she struggled to find time to complete the tasks that were continually added to her list of responsibilities.

The next day, Cassie arrived early to make sure everything was ready for the probability lessons. The first lesson would begin at 9:10 A.M., leaving her with nearly 2 hours to prepare. First, Cassie did a quick inventory to make sure she had all the supplies she would need: dice, playing cards, plastic beads, worksheets, and computers. She made photocopies and checked with the technology teacher to make sure all the computer stations were operating. Next, Cassie set out to talk with each of the teachers for whom she would model. En route, she popped into the office to check her mailbox, where she found the principal, Mr. Frank. He excitedly told Cassie about his idea for a Learning Carnival and they enthusiastically agreed that it would be a great activity for Cassie to plan next year. A parent in the office handed Cassie a pan of brownies for the faculty lounge and a teacher asked for Cassie's assistance with a shirt-painting activity later in the day. Another teacher approached to discuss the collection of student permission slips so that Cassie could videotape a Trailblazers lesson next week. Cassie addressed each of these issues in quick succession and then set out to find the classroom teachers.

By the time Cassie talked with all five teachers, her excitement about the probability lesson had almost completely disappeared. To her great disappointment, Cassie learned that none of the teachers planned to stay in the room when Cassie modeled the lesson. While frustrating, this lack of teacher involvement was not surprising. All year Cassie had tried unsuccessfully to collaborate with the teachers. She organized "pod" meetings for groups of grade-level teachers and offered to lead collaborative lesson planning sessions—in both cases teachers responded with apathy or outright resistance. Cassie had hoped that today's probability lessons would show teachers the value of constructivist approaches to math instruction and that she might finally start to build collaborative relationships with teachers. "At least the children will receive one constructivist math lesson," she told herself, trying to look on the bright side.

Returning to her office to collect the probability materials, Cassie found a stack of boxes along the wall with labels that read "test booklets," reminding her that next week she would serve as the testing coordinator for the state's standardized exams. Just then Mr. Frank appeared with a stack of Individualized Education Plans for Cassie to collate. Happy to be helpful to someone, if not to the teachers, Cassie accepted the paperwork and headed off to teach the first of five probability lessons.

In Sum

Cassie's experiences demonstrate how an ambiguous job description can result in the teacher leader assuming noninstructional duties. By taking on administrative and managerial duties, the purpose of Cassie's role is blurred, exacerbating the challenge of developing trusting relationships with teachers. Research on instructional teacher leadership indicates that teachers are more likely to seek instructional assistance from teachers than from administrators (Supovitz, 2008). To the extent that teacher leaders align themselves with administrative roles, they are less likely to serve as an instructional resource for teachers.

VIGNETTE 6. WORK WITH OTHER SCHOOL LEADERS: BEVERLY

Beverly Hughes worked as a literacy coordinator for grades four through eight in Johnson Elementary. In this vignette we learn about the challenges she faced in her working relationship with another teacher leader in the school, the literacy coordinator who worked with teachers in grades K–3.

Conflicting Roles

It was 6:30 A.M. on Monday morning and Beverly Hughes was already in her office at Johnson Elementary School. She looked carefully over her schedule for the week, a combination of demonstration lessons, observations, and grade-level professional development sessions with teachers. After making a few changes in the plan for the week, she focused on the observation she had scheduled that morning in a fifth-grade classroom. Beverly looked over Mrs. Alston's lesson plans. She noted the objectives of the lesson and compared them to lessons she had observed in Mrs. Alton's room in the past. Beverly jotted a few questions in the margins of the plan and noted two foci for her observation. She then walked to Mrs. Alston's room for a pre-observation conference carrying two cups of coffee.

After the observation, the pair debriefed the lesson Beverly had just observed. "During the literature circles, you might consider stepping back a little and letting the students play more of the leadership role," Beverly told Mrs. Alton, who hesitated for a moment, looking puzzled. "What is it?" Beverly asked, concerned. "Deidre told me in the professional development session that the two of you thought I should provide more structure, intervene more," she stated, looking uncomfortable. Beverly felt herself growing angry. "I will talk with Deidre about this," she told Mrs. Alton. "In the meantime, try pulling back just a little." Mrs. Alton nodded, looking at the floor.

Beverly was the literacy coordinator for grades four through eight at Johnson Elementary. She had been the literacy coordinator for 5 years. Prior to that, she taught in grades four through six for 18 years at several schools. An important aspect of Beverly's role was working with her colleague Deidre Ladson, the literacy coordinator for teachers in grades K–3. The two performed parallel roles in the school, and their mentoring aimed to reach all teachers in the building. Initially, Beverly was the only literacy coordinator and worked with teachers in all grades. The workload of mentoring all teachers in the large school proved to be impossible. In addition, Beverly had spent her entire career as a middle-grades teacher and, as a result, the primary teachers were less receptive to her mentoring. Beverly expressed her concerns to the principal, who created two coordinator positions, one for grades K–3 and one for grades 4–8. Deidre was hired to work with the teachers in the lower grades. While this improved Beverly's workload, her relationship with Deidre was strained.

Beverly felt her heart start to beat faster as she approached the office she shared with Deidre. When she entered, she saw that Deidre was debriefing a lesson with Mrs. Hegstrom, a second-grade teacher. Beverly sat at her desk with her back to Deidre and waited, rehearsing in her mind what she would say. A few minutes later, Mrs. Hegstrom got up to leave, nodding to Beverly as she walked out of the room. For a moment, Beverly didn't say anything. She finally turned to Deidre and asked if the two could talk. "I am pretty busy right now, is it important?" Deidre asked without looking up from her desk. Beverly hesitated for a moment but then said, "Yes, I think it is." Deidre sighed and rolled her eyes but she turned to face Beverly. "What?" she demanded. Beverly asked Deidre about the advice she gave Mrs. Alton. A brief, angry exchange followed. Deidre stormed out, slamming the door behind her.

Beverly sat at her desk, her hands shaking. She felt like she understood her position well. She was comfortable with the books, lesson plans, assessments, and literacy strategies she was supporting in classrooms. She had developed relationships of trust with the teachers. She didn't know what to do about her relationship with Deidre.

In Sum

Beverly's story highlights the interaction of instructional teacher leaders with staff in other leadership roles in their school and the influence of such relationships on the work they do. The kindergarten-through-third-grade literacy coordinator role was created from an existing role as Beverly's role was divided into two parts. Research demonstrates that role creation and role change are "deeply challenging work for the individuals so engaged" (Davidson, 2003, p. 745). Instructional leaders face the daunting challenge of defining the boundaries of their roles and negotiating interaction with other roles. They must work to define their role and situate it within the operating assumptions and culture of the school.

VIGNETTE 7. WORK WITH THE PRINCIPAL: LUCY

In this vignette Lucy, the literacy facilitator at Forbes Elementary School, faced challenges in her relationship with the school's principal. The literacy facilitator found herself at odds with the principal's new approach, which was stimulated by the pressures of high-stakes accountability.

From Autonomy to Control

Lucy called the third-grade-level meeting to order. It was a cold day in January, and the four teachers huddled together in Lucy's office for their early-morning meeting. Lucy led the teachers through a review of their grade-level goals for the second semester, which would begin in a few days. "Now, how do these goals fit in with the objectives we generated in the activity with the consultant Principal Lawson brought in?" Mr. Levine asked. Lucy contemplated her response for a moment, wanting to be respectful of Principal Lawson while still maintaining the integrity of the grade-level goal-generating process. "I think we can find ways to make the goals your grade level brainstormed and the objectives from the external consultant activity coherent," Lucy responded. As the grade-level meeting ended, she wondered if this was possible and if she was being honest.

Lucy was the literacy facilitator at Forbes Elementary School. Formerly she had been a third-grade bilingual education teacher at the same school for more than 15 years. This was her 3rd year as the literacy facilitator. Because she worked at a large school with more than 25 teachers, Lucy considered individual teacher mentoring to be impossible to undertake in an equitable way. As a result, she primarily spent her time in grade-level meetings and staff development workshops, where she worked with groups of teachers in each of the three grade areas: primary (K–3), intermediate (4–6), and upper grades (7–8).

In her previous 2 years as literacy facilitator, Lucy had autonomy in creating grade-area meeting agendas. Working collaboratively with teachers, they identified goals for improvement and created an improvement plan for each grade. The plan included grade-level meeting topics across the year designed to reflect the overarching improvement goals. Lucy was very proud of this collaborative approach and felt that teacher buy-in was high. Although in a few grade areas she disagreed with the teachers on some of the improvement area priorities, she felt that this tradeoff was worthwhile given the higher ownership on the part of the teachers.

After several years of improving test scores, the previous year the average achievement for the school had declined in both literacy and mathematics. Principal Lawson became very concerned and circulated a memo to all school staff members stating that "controls would be tightened." As the new school year opened, it became evident that Principal Lawson would take more control over Lucy's work. Principal Lawson began to set the grade-level meeting agendas. They were generated the week of the meetings. To Lucy, the topics seemed disjointed and largely focused on standardized test preparation. Similarly, the principal announced her intention to provide agendas and materials to Lucy for the grade-area staff development meetings. In addition, Lucy would only lead half of the grade-area meetings and external presenters would be hired to present at the other half. The topics would be largely focused on test preparation.

Lucy decided to meet with Principal Lawson to talk about the incoherence between the grade-level work and the work of the external consultants.

She caught Principal Lawson in the hallway outside the main office. "Can we talk?" Lucy asked. Principal Lawson nodded and invited Lucy into her office. Lucy explained the difficulties she was having integrating the grade-level goals and the objectives generated with the external consultant. She emphasized the importance of the grade-level goal-setting process, which empowered the teachers and created coherence in the improvement efforts within and across grades. "I feel I have made significant progress in improving the school through these grade-area meetings," she explained to Principal Lawson. "I don't want that to be short-circuited by these new improvement initiatives." She showed Principal Lawson her analysis of the test score dip. "It primarily occurred only in third and fifth grade," she explained, pointing at the numbers. "I think with some attention to those grade levels we can stay the course with what we are doing." Principal Lawson responded, "Are you suggesting that I was too hasty in the changes I made?" Lucy sat quietly for a moment. "I am not here to criticize you, Maria, I just want to talk about how the changes are affecting my role." Principal Lawson put her hand on Lucy's shoulder. "You know I respect you, Lucy, and your work. But what we were doing was clearly not working. Now it is time to try something new."

In Sum

Lucy's story demonstrates the challenges that can arise in the relationship between instructional teacher leaders and principals. Under pressure to improve standardized test scores, Principal Lawson and Lucy disagreed about the best way to proceed with the literacy program. Research on instructional teacher leadership indicates the importance of a strong working relationship between the teacher leader and the principal (Mangin, 2007). When principals are knowledgeable about the work that teacher leaders do and interact regularly with the teacher leader about matters of instruction, they are more likely to provide support to the teacher leader.

VIGNETTE 8. INFLUENCE OF SCHOOL NORMS AND STRUCTURES: ABBY

This vignette focuses on Abby, a literacy coach at West Elementary. The case explores the manner in which existing school norms and structures influence the implementation of instructional teacher leadership roles.

Fitting In

Abby sat at the table at the weekly fourth-grade level meeting. Working in pairs, the teachers discussed the most recent round of peer observations. Abby joined Mrs. Otis and Mr. Randell as they talked together about Mrs. Otis's observation of Mr. Randell's class.

"I was impressed with your overall management of the class, especially Tyrone," Mrs. Otis said, smiling.

"Yes, he can be a handful. Keeping him on task is difficult at times," Mr. Randell responded, smiling and shaking his head.

"I thought you did very well with that," Mrs. Otis reiterated.

As the two teachers talked, Abby listened intently to the discussion, taking notes. She occasionally nodded or smiled.

"Now, my suggestions for improvement focus on the class discussion portion of the class," Mrs. Otis added. "I am concerned that so few of the students participated." Mrs. Otis continued, providing Mr. Randell with some suggestions on how to discreetly engage and involve the quieter students.

Mr. Randell nodded and took notes as she spoke. Abby tried to make eye contact with the pair of teachers. She was ready to participate and make a comment. The two continued to talk, engaged in their conversation. Abby finally raised her hand and cleared her throat.

"Yes?" Mrs. Otis asked.

"You could also try small groups or pairs instead of full-class discussion," Abby added.

The two teachers looked at Abby for a moment and then returned to their conversation without responding to her suggestion. Abby didn't speak again during the meeting.

Abby had been the literacy coach at West Elementary for 2 years. She was a relatively inexperienced teacher when she took the position, having taught in second grade for 3 years. She was selected for the position because she had large test score gains in her classroom for 2 of the 3 years she was a teacher. Thus far, she has had little success gaining access to most classrooms. "I offer and offer, but there is little interest in anything I have," Abby wrote in her reflection journal. "I offer co-teaching, I offer demonstration, I offer materials. They take the materials and that is about all."

The principal at West Elementary, Ms. Parker, had been the principal for 18 years. Of all of her accomplishments, she was most proud of her grade-level meeting structure. For 10 years, Ms. Parker had worked to build strong grade-level teams. She reorganized classrooms so that grade-level teachers were situated near one another. She reconfigured the time schedule to make it possible for grade-level teachers to have shared meeting time every week. She positioned formal teacher evaluations within grade levels, adding a peer review component to the annual teacher review process.

Abby continued her day, moving from one grade-level meeting to the next. She generally sat quietly at the tables, taking notes and nodding as the teachers conversed. In the grade-level meeting for second grade, she arranged an observation in Mrs. Kinney's class for the following morning. "I am struggling with managing learning centers," Mrs. Kinney told Abby. "I am hoping you can give me a few suggestions." Abby nodded eagerly, taking notes to help her plan for the session. As a new teacher, Mrs. Kinney was more receptive to Abby's work. In the other grade-level meetings, Abby found the agenda full and the conversations steady and excited. "The meetings are functioning well," she wrote in her reflection journal. "There is just no place for me and my role."

While Ms. Parker interpreted the grade-level structure positively, Abby found that the strength of this structure impeded her from doing her work as literacy facilitator. "I feel like the add-on reform," she confided. "The grade-level teams are so efficient they don't need me," she wrote in her journal. Abby perceived the grade-level structures with mixed feelings. "Ms. Parker has successfully changed the school in a positive way and that is good," she stated. "But I am in a position where my role doesn't fit the culture. How can I possibly succeed?"

In Sum

In this vignette, Abby struggled to implement her role when the functions were in conflict with preexisting school norms. Research demonstrates that deep institutionalization of teacher leader roles is more likely to occur in schools where the school norms are in harmony with the assumptions underlying the role (Stoelinga, 2008). In a school where norms and processes existed for grade-level colleagues to help one another improve instruction, the purpose of the instructional teacher leader role was unclear to both Abby and the teachers.

VIGNETTE 9. THE TEACHER LEADERS' SKILLS: TARA

This vignette introduces Tara, a curriculum coordinator turned literacy coach at Brown Elementary School. Tara discovered she lacked important skills to do her job. As she worked to improve her skills, she struggled to convince teachers with whom she worked that she had what it took to do her job well.

A New Role

It was Tuesday, the day of the week that filled Tara with trepidation—the day she spent observing teachers' classrooms, providing them with feedback on literacy instruction. Tara nervously looked over her schedule of observations for the day. The 1:00 observation was in Ms. Bell's Room 305, she noted with a sigh. Ms. Bell was among those teachers most resistant to her observations and comments.

Tara had been a classroom teacher for 13 years at Brown Elementary School. She taught second and third grade for the majority of her career and was hired as the school's curriculum coordinator 4 years ago. Last year, because of the school's low academic performance, the district mandated the creation of a reading coach position in the school and Tara was reassigned to fulfill the new role. As the curriculum coordinator, Tara had primarily ordered, organized, and distributed instructional materials; she did not function as an instructional mentor. Tara did not consider herself to be an expert in literacy. In her new role, Tara was encouraged by district leaders to conduct regular observations of teachers and offer suggestions for how they might improve their instructional practice.

As she made her way to Room 103 for her first observation of the day, she saw Dr. Ortega, one of the district-level literacy coaches, in the hallway outside 103 waiting for her. A district literacy coach regularly observed Tara in her work. "I thought we might do some observations and debriefings with teachers together today," Dr. Ortega said, extending her hand to shake Tara's. Tara's hand trembled a bit as she extended her hand to meet Dr. Ortega's. She was not expecting a visit from the district coach today. The first three observations seemed to go well, Tara thought, as she and Dr. Ortega observed classes and then met with teachers afterward to discuss what they had observed. In the past, Tara had allowed Dr. Ortega to do most of the talking in teacher debriefing sessions. Today, Tara spoke out and made some suggestions. Dr. Ortega nodded along with Tara's comments, and Tara began to relax and enjoy her role a bit.

By the time the pair arrived at Room 305, Tara was feeling more confident about the observation of Ms. Bell. She considered warning Dr. Ortega that Ms. Bell was among the most resistant teachers to her work, but decided against it given the positive momentum of the morning. Ms. Bell's lesson began without incident. As they entered the room, Ms. Bell nodded to them and handed them the lesson she would be teaching. As she observed, Tara realized that Ms. Bell had modified the lesson, eliminating the small-group work and replacing it with whole-group instruction. She felt herself growing angry, as this was something that Dr. Ortega had explicitly told her was unacceptable in the literacy program. Dr. Ortega glanced at Tara, eyebrows raised. Tara shrugged back to her.

The students filed out and Ms. Bell, Dr. Ortega, and Tara sat down in chairs around Ms. Bell's desk for the debriefing. Dr. Ortega turned to Tara. "Why don't you start this debriefing, Tara?" she said. Tara was surprised, since Dr. Ortega had begun each of the three previous observation-conversations. Tara stumbled a bit as she collected her thoughts. "My biggest concern is that the lesson was modified to eliminate the small-group work . . ." she began. Ms. Bell crossed her arms tightly across her chest and interrupted Tara. "Dr. Ortega, I really trust your feedback and would like to hear from you rather than the curriculum coordinator," she stated, not looking at Tara. "In fact, I would prefer to talk with you alone." Tara felt the tears stinging in her eyes, especially at the description of her as "curriculum coordinator," and looked at Dr. Ortega. Dr. Ortega hesitated a moment and then asked her to leave the room. Tara was stunned that the district coach agreed to this and walked out. As she stood in the hall, tears streamed down her cheeks.

Several minutes passed before Dr. Ortega opened the door. She motioned for Tara to come back into the room. When they were all seated, it was silent for a moment. "Let's begin again, Tara, let's hear your comments on the lesson," Dr. Ortega stated. Tara hesitated and then began again, talking about the importance of small-group work and how it fit into the philosophy behind the literacy approach. Ms. Bell did not look at Tara but sat staring at her desk. When she finished, Dr. Ortega said, "That is enough for today." She shook Ms. Bell's hand and the two of them departed.

In Sum

Tara's story focuses on the qualifications and skills that are necessary for instructional teacher leaders to be successful in their role. Research suggests that certain knowledge and skills improve the work of instructional teacher leaders. For instance, the depth of teacher leaders' content knowledge affects their ability to influence instructional improvement and thus the overall effectiveness of teacher leader initiatives (Manno & Firestone, 2008). Instructional teacher leaders must also possess the procedural knowledge necessary to facilitate collective instructional improvement (Lord, Cress, & Miller, 2008).

Although research demonstrates that content and procedural knowledge can positively affect a teacher leader's level of instructional influence, the extent to which these skills are being developed is unclear. For example, only half of the teacher leaders that Manno and Firestone (2008) studied were content experts. Moreover, districts report that few applicants for teacher leader positions have the necessary combination of qualifications, prompting them to leave positions vacant (Camburn, Kimball, & Lowenhaupt, 2008) or to hire based on "willingness" rather than expertise (Mangin, 2008a). The complex content and procedural knowledge necessary for effective teacher leadership makes it difficult to find appropriately qualified candidates, potentially compromising their intended benefits.

Tara's story highlights the issues surrounding finding qualified candidates and providing essential training and support to instructional teacher leaders on the job.

Vignette Teaching Notes

ACTIVITY 1. EXAMINING ROLE FUNCTIONS

Objective: To understand the functions of instructional teacher leader roles as they are commonly conceptualized and enacted and in relationship to research on effective professional development.

In this activity we will examine the first three vignettes from Part 1 of this volume: Susan, Matt, and Stella. Together, these vignettes highlight a variety of role functions that are undertaken by instructional teacher leaders. The purpose of this activity is to build an understanding of the manner in which these functions are enacted and the objectives behind them. A secondary goal is to reflect upon the contexts within which instructional teacher leaders set goals and how goals might be matched to different situations.

Step 1: Identifying Role Functions across Cases

The first step in this activity is to identify the role functions that are evident in each of the three vignettes. Using Table 1.1 in the Appendix, mark the boxes that correspond to the functions described as part of each instructional teacher leader's role. To assist you, refer to Table 1.2 in the Appendix, which defines each function. This can be completed as an assignment for individual students or in small groups during class time.

Step 2: Discussing Role Functions in Small Groups

Work in small groups to discuss the functions that instructional teacher leaders undertake in the three vignettes. In your groups, discuss three questions:

1. Compare your matrices. Do you all agree on the functions that are described in each vignette? If not, discuss and attempt to reconcile the differences.
2. How does the school context influence the kinds of functions that the instructional teacher leader performs? Do some functions appear to be more appropriate for some contexts than others?
3. What other functions do the instructional teacher leaders perform that do not appear in the matrix? How might these functions detract from the goals of instructional teacher leadership? In what ways might these other functions be an appropriate extension of the teacher leader's work?

Step 3: Discussing Role Functions in Relation to Effective Professional Development

To understand the functions that instructional teacher leaders perform in relation to research on effective professional development, read:

Hawley, W. D., & Valli, L. (1999). The essentials of effective professional development: A new consensus. In L. Darling-Hammond & G. Sykes (Eds.), *Teaching as the learning profession: Handbook of policy and practice* (pp. 127–150). San Francisco: Jossey-Bass.

According to Hawley and Valli (1999) effective professional development: 1) is driven by learning goals and outcomes, 2) involves teachers in the identification of their learning needs, 3) is school-based, 4) is organized around collaborative problem solving, 5) is ongoing and includes follow-up support, 6) incorporates multiple sources of information on student outcomes, 7) provides opportunities to develop theoretical understanding of the knowledge and skills to be adopted, and 8) is integrated with a comprehensive change process. Adherence to these eight design principles can improve student achievement.

Work in small groups to discuss the chapter. Use the following queries to focus discussion:

1. What are the components of the eight design principles of effective professional development?
2. In general, how do the functions performed by instructional teacher leaders, as portrayed in Vignettes 1 through 3, compare to the eight design principles elaborated by the authors?
3. For each of the three instructional teacher leaders—Susan, Matt, and Stella—which design principles are most evident in the functions they perform? In what ways might the functions they perform be better aligned with the principles of effective professional development?

Modifications for Activity 1

Professional Development for Teacher Leaders. Using Table 1.1, ask teacher leaders to outline the role functions they perform in their own work. Have the teacher leaders estimate the amount of time they spend on each role function identified. How does this list of actual time spent compare with how they wish they spent their time?

Professional Development for Principals. Using Table 1.1, ask principals to outline the role functions that they consider ideal for a teacher leader in their school. After they outline these functions individually, ask principals to discuss the functions they selected in small groups. What are the primary goals for their instructional teacher leaders?

ACTIVITY 2: SCHEDULE OF TEACHER LEADER ACTIVITIES

Objective: To understand how the role functions of instructional teacher leaders are commonly scheduled and enacted.

In this activity you will examine the work schedules of the instructional teacher leaders highlighted in Vignettes 1 and 3, Susan and Stella. Examining their schedules will provide you with a deeper understanding of how these roles are enacted within schools.

Step 1: Analyzing Teacher Leader Schedules

The first step in this activity is to examine the sample coach schedules (see Tables 1.3 and 1.4, in the Appendix). The purpose is to establish the facts related to each teacher leader's schedule. Individually or in small groups, consider the following questions:

1. How much time does the instructional teacher leader dedicate to each function?
2. How many teachers does the instructional teacher leader interact with over the course of the week?
3. How much planning time does the instructional teacher leader use to perform her role?

Step 2: Discussing Teacher Leader Schedules in Small Groups

The second step is for small groups to discuss the teacher leader schedules. The purpose is to draw conclusions about how teacher leader functions are scheduled. Begin by considering each schedule on an individual basis and responding to the following questions:

1. What are the advantages of each schedule?
2. What are the disadvantages of each schedule?
3. What priorities are represented in each schedule?

Then look across the schedules and make comparisons. Consider:

4. In what ways are the two schedules similar?
5. In what ways are the two schedules different?

Finally, identify the schedule that you would endorse.

6. Explain your selection.
7. How is your selection influenced by your current role (teacher, administrator, instructional teacher leader) or your current work context?
8. What modifications would you make, if any, to deepen the work of the teacher leader?

Step 3: Designing a Teacher Leader Schedule

After completing Steps 1 and 2, design a teacher leader schedule. First, make choices about the design of the teacher leader's role. Identify: a) the subject area to be addressed, b) the size of the student and teacher populations, and c) the number of years the teacher leader role has been in place. As you create your schedule, make deliberate choices about the kinds of functions you will include and who they will target. Write a brief memo explaining the rationale behind your choices. Include:

1. A description of the teacher leader's goals.
2. An explanation for the selection of some functions over others.
3. An analysis of the strengths and weaknesses of the schedule.

Modifications for Activity 2

Professional Development for Teacher Leaders. Ask teacher leaders to write their own schedules based on what they do day-to-day. After completing this individually, have the teacher leaders meet in pairs to compare their schedules and to complete Step 3 above.

Professional Development for Principals. Ask principals to write the ideal schedule based on what they think a teacher leader in their school should do day-to-day. After completing this individually, have the principals meet in pairs to compare their ideal schedules and to complete Step 3 above.

ACTIVITY 3: EXPLORING CHALLENGES TO TEACHER LEADER
ROLE ENACTMENT

Objective: To explore the challenges that instructional teacher leaders face in the enactment of their roles.

Vignettes 4 through 9 focus on challenges that influence the work of instructional teacher leaders. The purpose of this activity is to explore the constraints that teacher leaders face as they enact their role.

Step 1: Identifying the Challenges

The first step in this activity is to identify the challenges that are discussed in Vignettes 4 through 9. The purpose is to develop an understanding of factors that constrain the work of teacher leaders.

On your own, make a running list of the factors that make the teacher leader's work more difficult. Next to each challenge on the list, note whether the challenge seems minor and easily resolved or major, requiring deliberate planning and significant changes. Then review your list of challenges with a partner. Have you identified the same challenging factors? Do you agree on the degree of challenge—minor or major? Discuss any differences in interpretation.

Step 2: Analyzing the Challenges

For this step of the activity you will work in small groups to analyze the challenges faced by instructional teacher leaders. Each group should focus on one vignette (from Vignettes 4 through 9).

To frame and inform your analysis, read:

York-Barr, J., Sommerness, J., & Hur, J. (2008). Teacher leadership. In T. L. Good (Ed.), *21st century education: A reference handbook* (pp. 12–20). Thousand Oaks, CA: Sage Publications.

Then, identify the primary challenge faced by the teacher leader in your vignette. Compare this challenge with what you have learned in the article. What do the authors tell us about the nature of this challenge? What are some possible solutions to this challenge?

Step 3: Presenting Challenges and Contemplating Solutions

Small groups will present their analyses in brief 5-minute synopses. Each presentation should include a summary of the challenges faced by the teacher leader, concepts from the article that help clarify the nature of the challenge, and potential solutions as outlined in the article or as interpreted by the group members.

Then, as a group, engage in a synthesizing discussion aimed at drawing conclusions across the vignettes. Consider the following queries:

1. In what ways do the challenges raised in the six vignettes overlap?
2. What supports seem critical to the successful enactment of teacher leader roles?
3. What might be done to lessen potential challenges prior to teacher leader role implementation?
4. How might challenges be addressed once the teacher leader role is in place?

Modifications for Activity 3

Professional Development for Teacher Leaders. Ask teacher leaders to write their own vignettes that reflect a pressing challenge that they are currently facing in their work. After they have completed their writing, teacher leaders can work in pairs to read one another's vignettes and discuss their challenges.

Professional Development for Principals. Engage in an extended discussion of Vignette 7, which focuses on the relationship between the teacher leader and the principal. Ask principals to write a continuation of the vignette to resolve the tension between Lucy and the principal. After they have completed their writing, ask principals to discuss the critical components of a successful relationship between an instructional teacher leader and a principal.

ACTIVITY 4: DEVELOPMENT OF A TEACHER LEADER JOB DESCRIPTION

Objective: To synthesize new understandings of instructional teacher leadership and to articulate that understanding in a clearly defined description of the instructional teacher leader role.

The previous three activities aimed to 1) deepen understanding of the functions of instructional teacher leader roles, 2) examine the scheduling and enactment of instructional teacher leader roles, and 3) explore the challenges that instructional teacher leaders face in the enactment of their roles. The purpose of this activity is to synthesize new understandings gained across these three previous activities and to demonstrate understanding through the development of an instructional teacher leader job description.

Step 1: Analyzing Instructional Teacher Leader Job Descriptions

The Appendix (Figures 1.1, 1.2, and 1.3) includes job descriptions of real instructional teacher leader positions that were posted in three different school districts. Assess the job descriptions in comparison to what you know about:

- The theory of action behind teacher leadership (see "Introduction").
- The kinds of activities teacher leaders perform, as demonstrated in Vignettes 1 through 3.
- The challenges that teacher leaders face in the enactment of their roles.

Step 2: Developing a Teacher Leader Job Description

You are an elementary school principal who has been given funding to create an instructional teacher leader position in either mathematics or literacy. Drawing upon your knowledge of the work of teacher leaders:

> Construct a job description to advertise for the teacher leader position in either mathematics or literacy. Your description should include a set of "required skills" and "main duties" that reflect the role functions the teacher leader will perform. Your design should reflect what you have learned in the vignettes.

Modifications for Activity 4

Professional Development for Teacher Leaders. Ask teacher leaders to write their own job descriptions based on what they do day-to-day. Have the teacher leaders complete Step 1 parts 1 and 2 above based on the description they have written of their own role.

Professional Development for Principals. Ask principals to write the job description of the teacher leader(s) in their schools. Have the principals complete Step 1 parts 1 and 2 above based on the description they have written of the role.

Activity 5: Individual Reflections on the Work of Instructional Teacher Leaders

The final closing activity for Part I is a short paper assignment to promote individual reflection on lessons learned about the work of instructional teacher leaders. In a four-to-five-page paper:

Part A: Describe the theory of action behind instructional teacher leader roles. How does the theory of action differ from past conceptualizations of teacher leadership?

Part B: Describe the role functions that make up the work of instructional teacher leaders. How can schedules be used to identify weakness in role enactment and to strengthen successful implementation of these roles?

Part C: Describe some of the challenges that instructional teacher leaders face in their role. How do these challenges limit the effectiveness of the role?

Part D: Reflect upon the work of instructional teacher leaders. What have you learned thus far? What questions remain unanswered for you about these positions?

Part 2

The Dilemmas of Instructional Teacher Leadership: Open-Ended Cases

The second Part of this volume contains five case studies. Each case presents a fundamental dilemma that teacher leaders encounter in their work. The dilemmas that we present fall into five categories, based on research:

1. Leading learning;
2. School norms and structures;
3. Relationships;
4. Principal support;
5. Data-based improvement.

Each case is followed by a set of notes, which include suggested readings and activities. The readings provide a lens for interpreting the case, and the activities facilitate the application of empirical research and theory. Together the cases, suggested readings, and activities provide the reader with a greater understanding of the dilemmas that instructional teacher leaders face and how to best respond to those dilemmas.

Open-Ended Case 1.
Leading Learning: Erin

This case highlights the high level of expertise needed to teach math and the steep learning curve it presents. Erin, the math lead at Mason Elementary, worked in a heavily unionized district located in the heart of a steel-mining region. The strong culture of traditionalism made changing educational practices a particularly daunting task in this district of nearly 3,000 predominantly White students. After reading and establishing the facts of the case, sociocultural adult learning theory will be used to frame the case and identify a set of strategies that Erin might use to facilitate teachers' learning.

A Slow Start

The knock at Erin's door came as a surprise. After all, it was Friday afternoon and most of the teachers had walked out to their cars with the students, not to mention that 3 months into her position as math lead, the teachers hadn't exactly been clamoring for Erin's help with the new Math Trailblazers program. Nevertheless, Mrs. Thompson, one of four second-grade teachers, stood just inside the door. She announced, "I thought you should know that the math lab, Rolling Along in Centimeters, didn't work. I did a double period on that lesson and in the end no one got it." Without missing a beat, Erin responded, "What part of the lesson didn't work?"

"I did everything just like I was supposed to," Mrs. Thompson replied. "I identified the problem for the students and told them that we would work on variables of 'type' and 'distance.' I explained that to find the answer we would use the middle value, which is easier than the average. Then, as a class, we rolled the cars down a ramp. I let each child take a turn rolling the car, but they took too long to measure so I did that part. Then I wrote all the values in a graph on the chalkboard. And finally I assigned the lab write-ups for homework. You should see what they wrote. They just don't get it."

Erin's head was spinning; she didn't know where to begin. She was relieved that a teacher finally wanted to talk with her about one of the math lessons. Erin's gut reaction was to say something positive and encouraging to Mrs. Thompson and reinforce the idea that the math lead is a source of support. Yet Mrs. Thompson's description of the lesson raised some red flags for Erin. Although she had never taught the Rolling Along in Centimeters lab, some of what she knew about constructivist math and the Trailblazers program didn't align with what Mrs. Thompson had described. For starters, it should have taken 4–5 days to complete the lab, which was intended to introduce students to the scientific method of mathematical problem-solving. In addition, it sounded as though Mrs. Thompson had walked the students through the experiment, providing step-by-step instructions. The whole point of the labs was for students to work on the investigation in pairs or small groups. Erin was shocked that Mrs. Thompson had done all the measuring, which left the students as passive observers. Even Mrs. Thompson's use of math terms such as "middle value" suggested that she herself might not fully understand the concepts of *mean, median,* and *mode.* In fact, Erin was so overwhelmed by what Mrs. Thompson had told her that she suggested they meet at a later date to discuss the lesson.

"I don't really want to discuss it. I just wanted you to know that it didn't work," replied Mrs. Thompson, who quickly turned and left. Feeling frustrated that she may have missed her opportunity, Erin also packed her bag, including the second-grade Math Trailblazers book. Over the weekend Erin would study the Rolling Along in Centimeters lab. She would also spend time thinking about how she might provide high-quality learning opportunities for teachers to gain deep understanding of mathematics.

The Math Lead Position

As the math lead for Mason Elementary School, Erin thought she had the best job ever. Three years earlier she had graduated from a local liberal arts college with a B.A. in elementary education. Her first teaching job had been at a K–2 elementary building in a district with a constructivist math program. Right from the start, Erin loved teaching math. Facilitating students' engagement in mathematical problem-solving was the most rewarding part of her work. Of course it had helped that Erin's colleagues took her under their wings, inviting her to watch them teach, helping her plan lessons, and providing feedback on her teaching. Erin knew she still had a lot to learn about math, but she had come to think of herself as specializing in math instruction. She had even joined the National Council of Teachers of Mathematics and attended their yearly conference. She enjoyed hearing about what other schools were doing and networking with teachers from outside her district.

After teaching for 3 years, Erin's husband was offered a new job on the other side of the state in Riverton School District. Riverton had very few openings for regular classroom teachers, but Erin had been intrigued by the description of the math lead position and decided to apply. At the interview, the assistant superintendent, Ms. Pert, explained that the Math Lead position was new. They were hiring three math lead teachers, one for each elementary school. The other two lead teachers had already been selected from the teaching staff. Unfortunately, none of the teachers at Mason Elementary had expressed interest in the position, so they were looking for an external hire. The main focus of the math lead would be to implement the constructivist program, Math Trailblazers. Ms. Pert emphasized that Erin wouldn't have any classroom responsibilities. Her main priority would be to serve as a resource for teachers. Ms. Pert thought Erin's prior experience with constructivist math and her youthful energy would be good for Mason Elementary.

To prepare Erin for the math lead position, Ms. Pert asked her to attend 4 days of Math Trailblazers training over the summer with the Mason Elementary teachers. "We want everyone to start with the same understanding—that the Trailblazers program is our top priority," Ms. Pert explained to Erin. On the first day of training Erin introduced herself to the teachers as the new math lead. Although she couldn't be certain, she thought she detected a chorus of raised eyebrows and sideways glances. "They don't know me yet," she reminded herself, "don't take it personally." During the lunch break Erin raised the idea of having an afterschool math club for students. She explained, "It will be a chance for teachers to work together to learn more about the Trailblazers materials and for students to receive supplemental instruction. We'll make it fun so students don't realize it's schoolwork." The silence at the table was finally broken by Mrs. Wren, who simply said, "We'll see." Quickly the teachers began to chatter about an upcoming presentation on pet care at the local bookstore, leaving Erin to wonder if math reform would be the teachers' top priority.

Three months later, Erin was certain that the Mason Elementary teachers did not share the district's commitment to math reform. Although the teachers dutifully taught the Trailblazers lessons, they managed to do so without changing their teaching strategies. Erin could hardly believe it, but the teachers transformed the Math Trailblazers lessons into teacher-centered direct instruction. Erin had offered to model constructivist teaching strategies to the teachers but they had rebuffed her, making no attempt to hide their disdain. "I've been teaching fourth grade for eighteen years," one teacher chided. "I really don't think I need a model lesson." Nevertheless, Erin was determined to offer teachers an opportunity to learn about the new math program. She spent much of her time studying the Math Trailblazers texts, trying to keep up with what each grade level was doing. Although teachers hadn't invited her into their rooms, she left weekly "Math Messages" in their mailboxes with helpful hints, additional resources, and reminders about supplies they would need to collect. Although she had never taught the Math Trailblazers program, its constructivist content was familiar and she felt confident that she would be able to assist the teachers when they felt ready.

Rolling Along in Centimeters

On the Monday morning following her conversation with Mrs. Thompson, Erin had not yet taken off her coat when second-grade teacher Mrs. Chianti approached her. "Erin, could you stop by my room after lunch? I looked at the lesson for today and it's a biggie. I'm not sure I have all the supplies. Well, I know I don't have the race cars. Anyway, could you help me set it up?" As Mrs. Chianti spoke, Erin felt herself nodding, telling the teacher that she'd swing by during lunch to make sure everything would be ready for the lesson. In her mind, Erin was shaking her head. She was amazed that the teachers still waited until the last minute to review the Math Trailblazers lessons when they knew the lessons required advance preparation. "On the other hand," thought Erin, "this is my chance to work with a teacher on the Rolling Along in Centimeters lab." Without wasting any time, she headed off in search of cars, ramps, measuring tape, and graphing paper.

During the lunch hour Erin found Mrs. Chianti in her classroom frowning at the Trailblazers workbook. Without looking up she grumbled, "I don't see why we're playing this car game when the kids haven't mastered their math facts yet. Usually at this time of year we play Math Bingo. That's a game. I don't see how racing cars is going to help them learn their math facts." Erin pressed her lips together, refraining from telling Mrs. Chianti about the educational benefits of constructivist math. Instead she offered, "Why don't you let me teach the lab today? I'd really like the practice. Afterward we can talk about how it went." To her surprise, Mrs. Chianti agreed, mumbling that she could use a break.

Minutes later the second-graders returned from lunch. Erin introduced herself to the students and explained that Mrs. Chianti was giving her a chance to practice a new kind of math where students would be in charge of running math experiments. "What does it mean to experiment?" she asked the children. "Turn to the person next to you and explain what an experiment is." As the lesson progressed, Erin grew increasingly confident that the students would be able to successfully complete the lab. Although it was clear that they hadn't spent much time working in groups or explaining their ideas to one another, they were all focused on math—something Mrs. Chianti also noticed. "I've never seen them this engaged, except when I have candy prizes for Math Bingo," she remarked.

After the 40-minute math lesson the children left for art class, giving Erin and Mrs. Chianti some time to talk about possible next steps. "That seemed to go pretty well," Mrs. Chianti conceded, "but they didn't get very far. Mrs. Thompson said she did this lesson in a double period. This looks like it will take all week." Hearing the tightness in Mrs. Chianti's voice, Erin quickly volunteered, "Why don't I come in every day this week to teach the lesson? You can watch and give me feedback." Mrs. Chianti agreed that Erin should probably finish what she had started, and together they decided that Erin would take responsibility for the math lesson throughout the week, including the materials.

Back in her office Erin did a victory dance, certain that her work as the math lead was about to snowball. In her mind she thought through a possible scenario: "Mrs. Chianti watches me teach and she realizes that I really am a great resource. Then she tells the other second-grade teachers, who decide to invite me to teach their students. Little by little I inch my way into each of the classrooms and model for all the teachers." As Erin considered the potential impact she could have on teachers' learning, she thought back to the mentoring she had received as a new teacher. "What was it about that experience that prompted me to grow as a math teacher?" she reflected. Quickly, Erin realized that the modeling her colleagues provided would have been ineffective if it hadn't been accompanied by other opportunities to learn. "The combination of watching one another teach, talking together about math instruction, examining student work together, and reflecting on how we could improve individually and collectively—that's what facilitated my learning." With that realization, Erin stopped her victory dance to sit down and map out a set of strategies she could employ to help facilitate teachers' learning.

Open-Ended Case 1 Teaching Notes: Case Analysis

ACTIVITY. CASE ANALYSIS

Objective: To analyze the case from the perspective of sociocultural adult learning theory. The analytical process will include three steps:

1. Establish the facts of the case.
2. Identify and define the problem.
3. Construct an appropriate response.

Each of these steps is elaborated below.

Step 1. Establishing the Facts of the Case

Begin by recalling the facts of the case using Table 2.1 in the Appendix as a guide. Through this process, establish what is known and unknown about the case. Be careful to distinguish between known facts and presumptions.

Further solidify your understanding of the case by comparing your list of facts with those of another classmate. Clarify and reconcile any areas of disagreement or inconsistency. When you feel confident that you know the facts of the case, proceed to Step 2.

Step 2. Identifying and Defining the Problem

The second step in analyzing the case is to identify and define the problem from the perspective of empirical research and/or theory. For this case, apply the analytical lens of sociocultural adult learning theory. Sociocultural adult learning is a field of study that examines social and cultural influences on learning as opposed to cognitive learning processes (as in the field of educational psychology). To learn about this theoretical perspective, read the two readings indicated below and engage in the accompanying activities.

READING 1

Bransford, J. D., Brown, A. L., Cocking, R. R., Donovan, M. S., & Pellegrino, J. W. (2003). Teacher learning. In J. D. Bransford, A. L. Brown, R. R. Cocking, M. S. Donovan, & J. W. Pellegrino (Eds.), *How people learn: Brain, mind, experience, and school* (2nd ed.) (pp. 190–205). Washington, DC: National Academy of Sciences.

This chapter, "Teacher Learning," describes the learning opportunities typically available to teachers and the quality of those learning opportunities. Most importantly, it outlines the kinds of learning opportunities that are most likely to facilitate adult learning.

Part 1. In small groups, consider the findings reported in this chapter and the implications for instructional teacher leadership in general using the following discussion questions:

1. What role might a formal instructional teacher leader play in providing high-quality learning opportunities for teachers?
2. What might this learning look like? What kinds of responsibilities, functions, and activities might it include?

Part 2. In a short paper (1–2 pages), apply the findings from the chapter to Erin's case to help identify and define the problem she faces in her role as math lead. In your paper, answer the following questions:

1. Based on what you learned in this chapter, what was the quality of Erin's learning opportunities when she was a new teacher?

2. Based on what you learned in this chapter, what challenge does Erin face in her role as math lead?

READING 2

Drago-Severson, E. (2006). How can you better support teachers' growth? *The Learning Principal*, 1(6), 1, 6–7.

This article offers a developmental perspective on adults as learners. The author identifies three distinct ways of knowing: *instrumental, socializing,* and *self-authorizing*. The different ways of knowing shape how adults engage in learning and can inform how school leaders provide effective opportunities to learn.

Part 3. In small groups, consider the findings reported in this article and the implications for instructional teacher leadership in general using the following discussion questions:

1. In general, how might instructional teacher leaders target the learning opportunities they present to teachers to best meet teachers' needs?
2. How can Erin incorporate theories of teachers' different ways of knowing into her work as the math lead?

Step 3. Constructing an Appropriate Response

To construct an appropriate response to the challenge that Erin faces, draw from the findings presented by Bransford et al. (2003) and Drago-Severson (2006).

Part 1. With a partner, design and describe a set of tasks that Erin might engage in over the course of the year. Chart the tasks in Table 2.2 in the Appendix, which identifies the task, target population, purpose of the task, how frequently it will occur, and the measures that will be used to evaluate Erin's progress.

Part 2. With a partner, use the protocol found in the Appendix (Table 2.3) to write a dialogue between Erin and Mrs. Thompson that would take place following the model lessons that Erin plans to provide. Interpret the dialogue in a running commentary (analytical notes) that you elaborate on the right-hand side of the paper. Be sure to capture Mrs. Thompson's "way of knowing" and the ways in which Erin responds.

Additional Reading Sources

To learn more about sociocultural adult learning theory, we recommend:

Bransford, J. D., Brown, A. L., Cocking, R. R., Donovan, M. S., & Pellegrino, J. W. (Eds.). (2003). *How people learn: Brain, mind, experience, and school* (2nd ed.). Washington, DC: National Academy of Sciences.

Drago-Severson, E. (2004). *Helping teachers learn: Principals' leadership for adult growth and development.* Thousand Oaks, CA: Corwin Press.

Drago-Severson, E. (2008). *Leading adult learning: Promising practices for supporting adult growth and development.* Thousand Oaks, CA: Corwin Press.

King, K. P., & Lawler, P. A. (2003). Trends and issues in the professional development of teachers of adults. In K. P. King & P. A. Lawler (Eds.), *New perspectives on designing and implementing professional development of teachers of adults* (pp. 5–13). [New Directions for Adult and Continuing Education, no. 98.] San Francisco: Jossey-Bass.

Open-Ended Case 2.
School Norms and Structures: Meg

This case introduces the ways in which school norms and structures influence the work that instructional teacher leaders do. Meg, a math coach, worked in a middle-income district with 6,000 students, 30% of whom were eligible for free and reduced-price lunch. Demographics in this suburban town had changed in the past 10 years, from 100% White to 45% African American and 15% Latino. Faced with cultural shifts and the need to strengthen and improve instruction, the district saw the math coach's assistance as vital for improvement efforts. After reading and establishing the facts of the case, research on professional communities and leadership will be used to interpret the case. This analysis will provide insights into the conditions underlying Meg's success and the challenges she faces.

Stepping into a New World

Driving toward Jefferson Elementary Meg rolled down the top on her white Chevy LeBaron, taking full advantage of the first day of warm weather. Although she had the radio on, Meg's mind was on today's fifth-grade team meeting at Jefferson Elementary School. Working with the Jefferson teachers this year had been one of the most rewarding experiences of Meg's career. She could hardly believe she had only worked in the Weston School District for 2 years.

The decision to come to Weston had been a difficult one. When she saw the posting for the math teacher trainer position she was already eligible for retirement in a neighboring school district. With 27 years of classroom experience and 4 years working as a school-level math coach, it seemed more likely that Meg would retire to her home at the shore than change districts and start all over again. But Meg still felt excited about math. She participated in math conferences, worked with the nearby university on math education research projects, and, most of all, loved sharing her passion for math with other teachers. When she learned that her math coach role would be reduced to part-time, Meg called Weston's assistant superintendent to see if the math teacher trainer position was still open.

Mrs. Feltz, Weston's assistant superintendent, couldn't believe her luck. They had been looking for someone to fill the new math teacher trainer position for 5 months. Although there had been a few internal applicants, none of them had the kind of expertise that Mrs. Feltz knew would be necessary. She wanted someone who really understood math concepts, someone who could help the teachers in Weston make the transition to more inquiry-based, constructivist teaching strategies. Making the switch would be a hard sell for many of the teachers, who were accustomed to more procedural, teacher-centered approaches to math instruction. Mrs. Feltz believed that a gifted trainer would be able to show teachers the value of concept-based math and help smooth the transition. Meg, she thought, would be perfect, not to mention that as an experienced coach and math expert, Meg would need very little oversight—a relief for Mrs. Feltz, who already had plenty to do.

The impetus for moving to a more concept-oriented approach to teaching math came from the new state standardized test, which included open-ended math questions and required students to explain their answers in writing. It was no longer enough to know *how* to solve an equation; students would have to explain their methods. In the first round of testing the Weston students had performed poorly. It was a shock to teachers and parents that their previously above-average children had become average overnight. In addition to the new test, the state had also released new math content standards. Teachers were told that if they covered the material outlined in the standards, the students would perform well on the exam. Although this sounded reasonable, teachers were struggling to figure out which lessons to teach. Their textbook included lessons that weren't part of the math standards and other standards were entirely missing, which meant that teachers would have to eliminate some lessons and add others. The past practice of starting with the first page of the textbook and working chronologically wouldn't be enough to cover all the necessary content standards.

To help smooth the transition, the school board voted to approve the use of general funds to hire a math teacher trainer who would provide professional development to teachers and help them align their instruction with the math content standards. The trainer's primary goal would be to improve student test scores by making sure that teachers were using methods that would improve student performance on the test. The math teacher trainer would work exclusively with teachers in grades 3–6 in each of Weston's four elementary schools—a total of 73 teachers.

Jefferson Elementary

Inside Jefferson Elementary Meg felt at home among the familiar noises of classroom hustle and bustle. Heading toward the teachers' workroom, she saw the principal, Susan Connors, walking toward her with a big smile on her face. Unlike Meg's relationship with the other elementary principals, which was limited to impromptu meetings in the hall, she met regularly with Principal Connors to discuss goals for math instruction and progress on student benchmarks. These conversations helped Meg plan her work with the teachers. As she drew near, Principal Connors exclaimed, "Oh, wonderful! The fifth-grade teachers are so excited to discuss what happened with the probability lessons. I think you'll be pleased. And I've got some good news, too. Stop by my office before you leave." Meg continued toward the workroom feeling confident that her work at Jefferson was appreciated.

Right from the start Meg's work with the Jefferson teachers had taken a different path from the other three schools. Meg had been pleased and surprised when Principal Connors invited her to visit the school before the teachers and students arrived in September so that they could discuss Meg's role. "I have been dreaming for this day to come," Principal Connors gushed. "My teachers are desperate for some quality learning experiences. I've tried to encourage them to coach one another, to form study groups, and to spend time in one another's classrooms. I really can't say a bad thing about my teachers, but truth be told, they don't know how to collaborate effectively." Principal Connors explained that the upper elementary teachers had requested weekly common planning periods, and she wondered if Meg would be willing to facilitate weekly grade-level meetings in addition to modeling occasional lessons. "Perfect!" agreed Meg.

That first year, working with the Jefferson teachers had been a dream. Meg focused on five mathematical topics—probability, discrete math, integers, fractions, and algebra. For each of the topics she followed the same steps. First, she created a binder of activities, lesson plans, and creative suggestions for teaching the topic using a concept-oriented, constructivist approach. Second, she modeled one of the lessons for each teacher. Third, she asked teachers to conduct a follow-up lesson from the binder. Fourth, the teachers convened in grade-level teams to discuss the lessons they had taught. Then, depending on each teacher's needs, Meg would either model the topic a second time or the teachers would continue on their own, sometimes holding a second discussion session.

The feedback that Principal Connors received from the teachers had been extremely positive. A fourth-grade teacher excitedly explained, "Meg showed me how to teach fractions in ways I had never thought of before." And a fifth-grade teacher told the principal, "I really struggled with algebraic language; I didn't even know what that meant. But after Meg modeled for me I had some concrete ideas for how to rephrase questions algebraically."

Unlike Jefferson, the other three elementary schools did not have common planning periods, and teachers seemed resistant to meeting before or after school. More than one teacher had briskly directed Meg to "just leave the stuff in my mailbox" when she tried to set up a meeting time. "If I can't bring teachers together to talk about math instruction, at least I can provide them with some materials," she thought. So Meg created three-ring binders for every teacher that included detailed information about which lessons to teach, which ones to exclude, and which replacement units should be added. As an added gesture, she developed all the replacement units herself and personally delivered them to each teacher. The task had been time-intensive, but Meg felt better knowing that all the teachers knew exactly what to teach. Informal feedback from the principals seemed to suggest that the teachers appreciated the replacement units, and Mrs. Feltz had been impressed that Meg had made contact with each and every teacher. She was even more excited when the test scores for upper elementary math increased that spring.

Now in her 2nd year as the math teacher trainer, Meg had deepened her work with the Jefferson teachers even further. After the success of the 1st year, Principal Connors suggested hiring substitute teachers to release teachers from class responsibilities and allow additional time to meet in grade-level teams. As a result, each of the upper elementary grades had an extended "lesson study" one afternoon of every month in addition to their weekly team meetings. The lesson study sessions included in-depth examination of math concepts, review of student performance, and visits to one another's classrooms. Although the lesson study sessions had been very popular with the teachers, Principal Connors cautioned Meg not to tell other administrators about the substitute-supported release time. She worried that they might disagree with her use of funds and want to restrict her autonomy over budgetary decisions. Meg was happy to keep quiet, confident that the teachers' best interests were being served. Besides, the other schools seemed content to see as little of Meg as possible.

Grade-Level Success

When Meg arrived at the teachers' workroom, five fifth-grade teachers were discussing how to adapt the textbook to align with the new math content standards. They quickly turned their attention to Meg, changing the conversation to the "You Bet" probability lesson that each of them had taught. As part of the lesson, students predicted the sums that would result if they rolled a pair of six-sided die 30 times. Students placed bets on the sums they thought would be more likely to occur. After seeing the outcomes, children were asked to explain why the probability of rolling some sums (such as 6) is greater than rolling other sums (such as 12). Meg listened to the teachers' reflections:

> *Kelly:* My children really enjoyed the lesson and I extended it to the level of having them evaluate and think about the likelihood of

getting different combinations. We used a set of dice at each table and that worked really well.

Tracey: We discussed what would be the probability of getting certain numbers. What number could you get? What number would be impossible to get? We also talked about what was fair and how could we make it unfair. They said you would have to change the rules. They were extremely involved and attentive.

Greg: I split them into two groups: ten and ten. And I changed the rules. I had them earning more points if they rolled certain numbers, such as the double numbers. So then I saw them putting chips on the double numbers. Then they discussed whether or not it was a good idea to bet on the double numbers.

For most of the 40-minute discussion Meg listened, offering modest advice when necessary. The teachers talked about how they could use the "You Bet" lesson as the basis for studying fractions. Greg noted that dice could be used as part of a multiplication lesson, helping students to identify all the factors of a given number. All of the teachers agreed that it would be useful to introduce dice-related lessons much earlier in the year. They finished the grade-level meeting by looking at some of the other lessons in the binder, and the teachers decided to try a card game that will continue the concept of probability and introduce fractions.

On her way to the principal's office, Meg thought about the amazing progress the fifth-grade teachers had made. Last year they had been reluctant to stray far from the textbook. Now they were more attuned to the learning process and less focused on getting through the book. Back in the main office, Principal Connors greeted her with a big grin and announced, "I wanted you to be the first to know. We got our state test scores back and the upper elementary scores went up ten percent!" Meg could hardly believe her ears. Of course she knew that the teachers had made great strides, but she was never quite sure their learning would be reflected in the students' test scores. She smiled to herself, imagining the tremendous sense of validation the teachers would feel when they heard the test results.

Meg's own sense of accomplishment was short-lived. There was an urgent message on her cell phone from Mrs. Feltz saying, "Meg, we need to talk. I got the test scores back and things don't look good. Three of the four schools' math scores dropped and the principals have been calling with questions. They want to know why Jefferson has been getting all the help. I'm afraid they are looking for someone to blame. I need you to come in right away so we can do damage control. I'll be especially interested in hearing your side of the story. I just don't understand why you would stop working with three-quarters of the teachers and never mention it to me." Starting the engine, Meg thought wryly, "Maybe it is time to retire."

Open-Ended Case 2 Teaching Notes: Case Analysis

Activity. Case Analysis

Objective: To analyze the case using research on professional communities and leadership. The analytical process will include three steps:

1. Establish the facts of the case.
2. Identify and define the problem.
3. Construct an appropriate response.

Each of these steps is elaborated below.

Step 1. Establishing the Facts of the Case

Begin by recalling the facts of the case, using Table 2.1 in the Appendix as a guide. Through this process establish what is known and unknown about the case. Be careful to distinguish between known facts and presumptions.

Further solidify your understanding of the case by comparing your description of the facts with those of another classmate. Clarify and reconcile any areas of disagreement or inconsistency. When you feel confident that you know the facts of the case, proceed to Step 2.

Step 2. Identifying and Defining the Problem

The second step in analyzing the case is to identify and define the problem from the perspective of research on professional communities and leadership. To learn about these two bodies of research, read the two articles indicated below and engage in the accompanying activities.

Reading 1

Kruse, S., Louis, K., & Bryk, A. (1994). *Building professional community in schools*. Madison, WI: Center on Organization & Restructuring Schools.

A school-based professional community is characterized by norms of professional behavior. This article describes the five critical elements (norms) of professional communities and the conditions that facilitate such communities. The authors explain that professional communities require supportive structural conditions as well as appropriate social and human resources. For this case, focus your analysis on the critical elements of professional communities and the necessary structural conditions. (Social and human resources will be analyzed in Open-Ended Cases 3 and 4 in this volume.)

Part 1. First, consider the implications for instructional teacher leadership in general. On your own, write briefly about the following question:

> What role might a formal instructional teacher leader play in the development of professional communities?

Part 2. In small groups, share your written reflections from Activity 1 above. Then work as a group to apply what you know about professional communities to Meg's case to help you make sense of her role as math teacher trainer in the Weston School District:

1. Which critical elements of professional communities were evident at Jefferson Elementary?
2. What kinds of structural conditions were in place at Jefferson Elementary? And how did these structures support the critical elements of professional community?
3. What was Meg's role in the development of professional community at Jefferson Elementary?
4. How did the other three elementary schools differ from Jefferson? How did those differences lead to differential enactment of the math teacher trainer role?
5. From the perspective of research on professional communities, what challenge does Meg face in her work as a math teacher trainer?

READING 2

Johnson, S. M., & Donaldson, M. L. (2007). Overcoming the obstacles to leadership. *Educational Leadership*, 65(1), 8–13.

Johnson and Donaldson summarize a list of obstacles to the successful implementation and enactment of instructional teacher leadership. The authors argue that in order to be successful, teacher leaders must overcome constraints created by school culture including autonomy, egalitarianism, and seniority.

Part 3.

1. Using Table 2.4 in the Appendix as a guide, assess the extent of the existence of the barriers described by Johnson and Donaldson at

Jefferson. Using the first two columns in the table, note whether the obstacles existed at Jefferson and the strategies used to overcome the obstacles as evidenced in the case.

Part 4. In small groups, complete the activities below:

2. Compare your assessment of each barrier using your tables. Do you agree in your interpretation of the obstacles and the strategies used in the case to overcome them? Talk through any areas of disagreement.
3. Work together to identify ways to improve the strategies utilized in the Jefferson case, filling in the final column of Table 2.4 together.

Step 3. Constructing an Appropriate Response

To construct an appropriate response to the challenge that Meg faces, draw from the findings presented by Kruse, Louis, and Bryk (1994) and Johnson and Donaldson (2007). One way of stating the challenge that Meg faces might be to ask:

How can Meg facilitate the dual goals of developing professional community and providing effective professional development in the four elementary schools?

Part 1. Imagine that you are a principal at one of the "other" elementary schools. After speaking with Principal Connors about how she leads her school, you decide that your school is due for some changes. Begin by writing a set of goals for your school, the faculty, and yourself that you would like to work toward.

Part 2. Write a letter to Mrs. Feltz from Meg's perspective. Explain your rationale for enacting the role of math teacher trainer as you did. Conclude by suggesting some changes for the upcoming school year that will better align with the district's goals. To support your ideas, provide evidence from research.

Additional Reading Sources

To learn more about research on professional communities, we recommend:

Kruse, S. D., Louis, K. S., & Bryk, A. (1995). *Professionalism and community: Perspectives on reforming urban schools.* Thousand Oaks, CA: Corwin.
Lieberman, A. (Ed.). (1988). *Building a professional culture in schools.* New York: Teachers College Press.

Louis, K. S., & Marks, H. M. (1998). Does professional community affect the classroom? Teachers' work and student experiences in restructuring schools. *American Journal of Education, 106*(4), 532–575.

Louis, K. S., Marks, H. M., & Kruse, S. D. (1996). Teachers' professional community in restructuring schools. *American Educational Research Journal, 33*(4), 757–798.

To learn more about leadership, we recommend the following materials:

Mangin, M. M., & Stoelinga, S. R. (Eds.). (2008). *Effective teacher leadership: Using research to inform and reform.* New York: Teachers College Press.

Smylie, M. A. (1997). Research on teacher leadership: Assessing the state of the art. In B. J. Biddle, T. L. Good & I. F. Goodson (Eds.), *International handbook of teachers and teaching* (pp. 521–592). Boston: Kluwer Academic Publishers.

Smylie, M. A., Conley, S., & Marks, H. M. (2002). Exploring new approaches to teacher leadership for school improvement. In J. Murphy (Ed.), *The educational leadership challenge: Redefining leadership for the 21st century; 101st yearbook of the National Society for the Study of Education* (Vol. 101 pt. 1, pp. 162–188). Chicago: University of Chicago Press.

Tschannen-Moran, M. (2009). Fostering teacher professionalism in schools: The role of leadership orientation and trust. *Educational Administration Quarterly, 45*(2), 217–247.

York-Barr, J., Sommerness, J., & Hur, J. (2008). Teacher leadership. In T. L. Good (Ed.), *21st century education: A reference handbook* (pp. 12–20). Thousand Oaks, CA: Sage Publications.

Open-Ended Case 3.
Relationships: MaryAnn

This case introduces the influence of relationships on the work of instructional teacher leaders. MaryAnn was a literacy coach at Maribel Elementary, a K–8 school located in a large urban district. Maribel was a diverse school serving 650 predominantly Latino students with a small group of African American and Asian students, the vast majority from low-income backgrounds. Maribel was also a school in which norms of privatized practice dominated, making it difficult for MaryAnn to develop relationships with teachers. After reading and establishing the facts of the case, research on micropolitics of education and theories of relational trust will be used to interpret the case and identify a set of strategies that MaryAnn might use to improve her work.

Reaching Out

The sun was just beginning to rise as MaryAnn arrived at Maribel Elementary. She pulled into a parking space facing the school building and sighed, staring at the building for a moment before turning off the car and gathering her materials for the fourth early-morning literacy workshop of the year. Would anyone come this morning? After sitting in the parking lot for some time, MaryAnn finally made her way into the building. She glanced at the clock in the hallway. The clock read 6:15 A.M. She had 45 minutes to set up and prepare for the workshop.

At 7:15 a set of literacy materials and caddies of markers, Post-its, and chart paper were on each table in the library. Coffee and donuts were arrayed on a table against the wall next to the entrance to the library. Classical music played softly on the CD player. No teachers had yet arrived for the 7:00 session. At 7:30, three teachers were at the tables. MaryAnn decided to begin the workshop despite the small numbers, given that she now only had 30 minutes left in an hour session. Another teacher arrived at 7:45. The other 20 chairs remained empty. MaryAnn rushed through the materials given the shortness of time. She struggled to modify the activities she had designed for small groups of five to six to use with four teachers. Two of the teachers engaged in the activities as best they could. The two worked together on creating Writers' Workshops for their fourth-grade classrooms. "Could you come to my classroom and observe the first time we try this?" one teacher asked MaryAnn. MaryAnn agreed, and the two looked through their calendars together. In contrast, the other two teachers were silent for much of the time, one with arms crossed and jaw set. "That may have been the longest half-hour of my life," MaryAnn told the principal and assistant principal a few hours later. "What do I do next?"

Making a Difference

MaryAnn had been in education for more than 25 years when the school district advertised a number of school-based literacy coach positions. The literacy reform was aimed at the lowest-performing schools in the district. Schools on probation were required to introduce a new approach to literacy and to designate a school-based literacy coach. A large cadre of literacy coaches was interviewed and selected in the 1st year of the reform. MaryAnn was selected as one of these first coaches.

MaryAnn saw the advertisement posted in the teacher's lounge of the elementary school where she had been teaching fifth grade and special education. She had been contemplating for some time what to do next in her career. Should she retire? Should she pursue a position in administration? While her position was comfortable and familiar, she no longer felt challenged. She longed to feel like she was learning new skills and wanted to share all that she had learned over the years with others. "I was in a high-achieving school with middle-class kids. I wanted to be working with students and teachers who needed me," she stated in the 1st week of her new position as literacy coach at Maribel Elementary. "I really want to make a difference in the lives of children who need it the most."

Maribel Elementary

Maribel Elementary is a school with historically low student achievement. Student scores on standardized assessments have placed Maribel in the bottom 5% of all elementary schools in the district. Maribel is located in an area of the city that has suffered a massive depopulation as jobs have become scarce, housing has deteriorated, and families have moved out. Two elementary schools within walking distance of Maribel closed, leading to an influx of students from different parts of the neighborhood, contributing to fights, disciplinary issues, and general chaos.

While these surrounding schools were closed due to underutilization, the influx of students made Maribel overcrowded, and every available space has been converted into classrooms, including the gym and auditorium. A similar influx of new teachers took place as the number of students increased.

"Old" and "new" faculty members conflicted, contributing to the distrust that already existed between staff members and between the faculty and the administration. At the same time, the "old" school staff was very senior and there was relatively low turnover. Many of these teachers had been at the school for their entire careers. In contrast, the principal position turned over repeatedly from contract to contract, giving the school a lack of stability in leadership.

Inroads to Success

Over 3 years, MaryAnn built relationships with a small group of teachers gradually, using a variety of approaches including providing materials, purchasing supplies for teachers, offering to provide demonstration lessons, building in-classroom libraries, and advocating for additional supplies from the principal. In the 1st year of her position, she mainly provided professional development sessions by grade level to all of the teachers. MaryAnn also led literacy professional development sessions at the school level during district in-service days.

In the 2nd year, MaryAnn felt she was making progress with a handful of teachers. She began offering demonstration lessons to model some of the literacy practices being taught in the grade-level workshops. MaryAnn also offered before-school and afterschool workshops, and arranged for participating teachers to get credits that would translate into raises in the district payroll system.

In the 3rd year, MaryAnn moved increasingly toward observations and co-teaching in the classrooms of the small group of teachers with whom she had been able to build relationships of trust. "After three years, I feel like I can dig into their practice with a critical eye and our relationship is strong enough to allow it," MaryAnn shared. "I could not say this about a single teacher in my first year in the position, so I see this as a huge accomplishment." At the same time, she continued to reach out to more resistant teachers using grade-level meetings and before- and afterschool workshops.

A few weeks after the fourth literacy workshop of the year, MaryAnn attended a district workshop for literacy coaches. One of the sessions focused on assessing her work with teachers. "To how many teachers in your building do you provide regular (at least once a month) mentoring services?" MaryAnn had never thought about her work quite this way. On the back of the form, she made a list of the teachers with whom she had worked at least once a month. She counted the teachers who had attended a before- or afterschool literacy workshop. She wrote on the form, "6 or 7." "What proportion of your school's teachers is this?" the next question on the form read. MaryAnn realized she had managed to build relationships with only about

25% of the teachers at her school. MaryAnn discussed her situation with five other literacy coaches in a small group at the district session. "I have worked so hard to reach the teachers I have reached that I feel good about the relationships I do have and the difference I have made," she stated to the other literacy coaches. "I hate having to think about it in terms of percentage because I feel it minimizes what I have accomplished," she continued. "But it is also a good reality check for me." Other coaches in MaryAnn's group shared similar experiences. "What do we focus on first, that seems to be the question everyone is asking," MaryAnn reflected. "How do I get my resistors on board?" she asked her colleagues.

Choosing a Path

It was Tuesday and MaryAnn was running late. She ran across the parking lot. She rarely arrived late to school. She had met a literacy coach from a neighboring school for breakfast to discuss common problems they were having in their role. As she entered Maribel, MaryAnn suddenly realized it was the first Tuesday of the month, the day when district literacy support staff always came to observe. What terrible luck! MaryAnn raced up the stairs toward her second-floor office, calling out several hurried hellos to colleagues as she passed them on the stairs. The district-level literacy coach, Emily Chalmers, was already waiting at her office. "I am so sorry to keep you waiting," MaryAnn panted. "I was just meeting with Rachel Elison to strategize about getting our teachers on board," she explained to Emily. "That is one of the issues I want to talk with you about today," Emily stated, nodding. MaryAnn and Emily entered her office together. MaryAnn glanced around, discouraged. Testing booklets from yesterday's practice session for the Iowa Test of Basic Skills were stacked on her meeting table. Materials to be distributed to teachers for classroom libraries littered the floor. "What a mess, I am so sorry," she told Emily. Emily looked concerned but stated, "It's okay, it's okay." The two worked together to stack the testing booklets on the floor and sat at the table. "Let's talk about your difficulties getting into classrooms," Emily said. "I have been turned away from many classrooms repeatedly, not being granted access of any kind, even to build a library or provide a demonstration lesson," MaryAnn responded. "In a small number of classrooms, I am welcomed, even sought out, while in many others, I have no access at all." Emily thought for a moment and then stated, "You need to pressure teachers to be on board."

Later that afternoon, MaryAnn met with Maribel's assistant principal, Lonnie Taylor. She shared with Lonnie Emily's suggestion that MaryAnn announce the school may be eligible for closing if it does not improve. "Emily thinks that telling the teachers the school might be closed will serve as motivation," MaryAnn said. Lonnie nodded slowly, looking upset. MaryAnn explained that Emily also offered to make these announcements at a staff meeting at the school, to provide some accountability. "I cannot decide if aligning myself with the district staff is a good idea, or if threats will help," she confided to Lonnie. "I fear it will only close teachers off even more. What do you think?"

Late into the evening, MaryAnn remained at her desk in her office, thinking. She felt both proud of and frustrated with her work. She knew she had made tremendous progress, and yet still she had not been able to reach the majority of teachers in her building. MaryAnn did not know what to do next. Should she focus on the teachers who wanted to work with her and hope that others would follow? Should she work with the principal to try to get additional support and accountability to work with teachers? Should she work with district staff to pressure the principal and teachers? MaryAnn realized with astonishment that it was after 7:00 P.M. and she still had to plan the demonstration lesson for Mrs. Laflin's class scheduled for tomorrow. "One day at a time," she thought and focused on preparing the lesson, pushing all else from her mind.

Open-Ended Case 3 Teaching Notes: Case Analysis

ACTIVITY. CASE ANALYSIS

Objective: To analyze the case using research on micropolitics of education and theories of relational trust. The analytical process will include three steps:

1. Establish the facts of the case.
2. Identify and define the problem.
3. Construct an appropriate response.

Each of these steps is elaborated below.

Step 1. Establishing the Facts of the Case

Begin by recalling the facts of the case using Table 2.1 in the Appendix as a guide. Through this process, establish what is known and unknown about the case. Be careful to distinguish between known facts and presumptions.

Further solidify your understanding of the case by comparing your description of the facts with those of another classmate. Clarify and reconcile any areas of disagreement or inconsistency. When you feel confident that you know the facts of the case, proceed to Step 2.

Step 2. Identifying and Defining the Problem

The second step in analyzing the case of Maribel Elementary is to identify and define the problem. In the analysis of this case, draw upon the analytical lens of the *micropolitics of education*. To learn about the micropolitics perspective, read the articles listed below and complete the related activities.

READING 1

Lindle, J. C. (1999). What can the study of micropolitics contribute to the practice of leadership in reforming schools? *School Leadership and Management, 19*(2), 171–178.

Jane Lindle describes and defines the micropolitical perspective in education, as a lens that takes into account the politics that take place in and around schools. Lindle uses scenarios to illustrate "the inherent political realities of schools" (p. 172).

Part 1. Lindle states that micropolitics "represents the networks of individuals and groups within and surrounding schools, who compete for scarce resources, even power" (p. 171). On your own and using Table 2.5 in the Appendix as a guide, outline the micropolitical reality at Maribel by answering the following questions:

1. The micropolitical perspective emphasizes the existence of individuals and groups in schools with conflicting or competing interests. What such *factions* are evident in Maribel Elementary?
2. What *characteristics or interests* define the boundaries between these groups? Note that powerful individual actors can be defined as an interest group and that an individual may be a part of multiple interest groups. Be sure to provide evidence from the case study for the identification of factions and their interests in the table.

Part 2. Work in small groups to complete the following:

3. Compare the summaries from Table 2.5. Talk through any differences in interpretation of the micropolitical summaries.
4. What are the sources of *conflict* evident at Maribel Elementary? What evidence can you find of competing values surfacing?

READING 2

Iannaccone, I. (1991). Micropolitics of education: What and why. *Education and Urban Society, 23*(4), 465–471.

Iannaccone emphasizes that the micropolitical perspective is focused on "processes for producing policy from conflict" (p. 467). From this viewpoint, attention must be paid to the interest groups within an organization, and to how conflicting values are introduced into and managed within a school.

Part 3. On chart paper, work as a group to visually depict the micropolitical picture of Maribel Elementary, drawing upon Table 2.5. Sketch the interest groups in the school and visually indicate conflict or cooperation between them.

Step 3. Constructing an Appropriate Response

To construct an appropriate response to the dilemma MaryAnn faces, you will draw upon the analytical lens of *social and relational trust*. Read Bryk and Schneider (2003). After you complete the article, work in small groups to complete the activities described below.

READING 3

Bryk, A., & Schneider, B. (2003). Trust in schools: A core resource for school reform. *Educational Leadership, 60*(6), 40–44.

In "Trust in Schools," Bryk and Schneider state that social trust among teachers, parents, and students improves schools. Social trust is built on relationships in which all participants have an understanding of his/her roles, and mutual dependencies to achieve organizational outcomes. The authors argue that such trusting relationships are built upon four specific concepts: respect, personal regard, competence in core role responsibilities, and personal integrity.

Part 1. With your partner, apply each of Bryk and Schneider's four key concepts—respect, personal regard, competence in core role responsibilities and personal integrity—to the case of Maribel Elementary. Together write one brief memo that includes two sections:

1. First, describe the state and extent of the four key concepts (four bullet points with one to three sentences each).

2. Second, offer a set of recommendations for addressing MaryAnn's situation (again, bullet points will suffice). Your recommendations should build on what you learned from reading Bryk and Schneider (2003). Memos should be approximately one to two pages in length.

Part 2. Assemble small groups of four (two pairs that each wrote a memo in Activity 4). Read one another's memos. Compare and contrast your application of the Bryk and Schneider framework and the recommendations. In your discussion, draw upon the visual representations you produced in Part 1 of Step 3.

Additional Reading Sources

To learn more about the micropolitics of education, we recommend the following materials:

Ball, S. (1987). *The micro-politics of the school: Towards a theory of school organization*. London: Methuen.

Blase, J. (1991). (Ed.). *The politics of life in schools: Power, conflict and cooperation* (pp. 120–130). Newbury Park, CA: Sage.

Blase, J. (1993). The micropolitics of effective school-based leadership: Teachers' perspectives. *Educational Administration Quarterly, 29*(20), 142–163.

Iannaccone, L., & Lutz, F. W. (1994). The crucible of democracy: The local arena. *Journal of Education Policy, 9*(5), 39–52.

Katz, M. B., Fine, M., & Simon, E. (1997). Poking around: Outsiders view Chicago school reform. *Teachers College Record, 99*(1), 117–157.

Malen, B. (1994). The micropolitics of education: Mapping the multiple dimensions of power relations in school politics. *Journal of Education Policy, 9*(5), 39–52.

Marshall, C., & Scribner, J. D. (1991). It's all political. *Education and Urban Society, 23*(4), 347–355.

Mawhinney, H. B. (1999). Reappraisal: The problems and prospects of studying the micropolitics of leadership in reforming schools. *School Leadership and Management, 19*(2), 159–170.

West, M. (1999). Micropolitics, leadership and all that . . . The need to increase the micropolitical awareness and skills of school leaders. *School Leadership and Management, 19*(2), 159–170.

To learn more about relational trust, we recommend the following materials:

Bryk, A. S., & Schneider, B. (2002). *Trust in schools: A core resource for improvement*. New York: Russell Sage Foundation.

Kramer, R. M., & Tyler, T. R. (Eds). (1996). *Trust in organizations*. Thousand Oaks, CA: Sage.

Payne, C. M. (2008). *So much reform, so little change: The persistence of failure in urban schools.* Cambridge, MA: Harvard University Press.

Raywid, M. A. (1995). Professional community and its yield at Metro Academy. In K. S. Louis & S. D. Kruse (Eds.), *Professionalism and community: Perspectives on reforming urban schools* (pp. 45–75). Thousand Oaks, CA: Corwin Press.

Open-Ended Case 4.
Principal Support: Jeff

This case introduces the role that principals play in the enactment of instructional teacher leadership. Jeff worked as the math lead teacher for two elementary schools in Valley School District, which served approximately 6,000 students in a densely populated region marked by industry, manufacturing, and shipping. The ethnically diverse district had experienced recent declines in student test scores and there was increased pressure to boost measurable student achievement. After reading and establishing the facts of the case, research on the principal's role in supporting effective teacher leadership will be used to interpret the case and identify a set of strategies for increasing the support Jeff receives from Principal Weaver.

Taking Stock

Jeff hesitated before pressing the "print" button on his computer. His eyes scanned the list of 12 names—exactly half the teachers in Westin Elementary School. For the umpteenth time he wondered, "Maybe I should just include all the teachers," but then reminded himself, "Principal Weaver specifically asked for a list of teachers I have worked with this year in my capacity as math lead teacher." Jeff knew it would be stretching the truth to say he had worked with all the teachers. Technically, they all heard his monthly report at the faculty meeting, but only 12 had met with him to discuss issues related to math instruction. Even then, some of the interactions had been brief and only nominally focused on math instruction. In good conscience, he couldn't list the entire staff. At the same time, Jeff worried about the consequences of providing the principal with a list of teachers' names. Would Principal Weaver accuse him of not working hard enough? Would he reprimand teachers whose names were not on the list? What would teachers say when they found out that Jeff had provided the list of names to Principal Weaver?

As Jeff watched the paper scroll from the printer, he felt the familiar feeling of agitation that seemed to strike every time he thought of Principal Weaver. "All year he barely says hello and now he wants a report on what I've done," Jeff grumbled to himself. Jeff knew that the school board had asked all the principals to report on their supplemental programs at tonight's board meeting. The value of the math lead teacher role would be scrutinized in light of budget restrictions. Jeff worried that Principal Weaver knew too little about the role to answer the board's questions. What if he lost his job due to Principal Weaver's lack of involvement? "At least Principal Malen will be there," Jeff thought with some relief. "She knows exactly what I do—without having to ask me for a list of names."

Valley School District

Jeff had been a math lead teacher for two and a half years. His role was split evenly between two schools: Westin Elementary and Portland Elementary, both serving grades K–4. The two schools were similar in their demographics and composition. Both had roughly 35% African American students, 35% White students, and 25% Hispanic students. Approximately 10% of the students were English Language Learners and 45% were eligible for free and reduced-price lunch. The turnover rate in teachers was about 15% each year, including teacher retirements, and about half the teachers were residents of the Valley School District.

The socioeconomic status of the student population made the Valley School District eligible for a number of supplemental grants as well as state and federal monies. After having success with a literacy lead teacher role, the school board approved the development of two math lead teacher roles. Jeff had been an obvious choice for one of the positions, given his 12 years of teaching experience in the district and his special love of math. In the past, Jeff had been asked to consider an administrative position, but he was leery of getting too far away from the classroom. The math lead position seemed like the perfect alternative.

New Role—New Relationships

In anticipation of his new role as math lead, Jeff spent the summer planning all the ways he would provide resources and assistance to teachers. Jeff imagined working with individual teachers to increase their knowledge of math concepts. He pictured himself facilitating grade-level conversations about teaching strategies. He saw himself examining student work with a team of teachers to identify areas for improvement. Jeff was even excited about organizing staff development days!

What Jeff hadn't imagined was the relationship he would have with the two school principals. In fact, he hadn't considered the principals at all. In Jeff's 12 years of teaching at Westin, Principal Weaver had always granted teachers the autonomy to teach as they saw fit. Principal Weaver prided himself on having a "teacher-run school" in which empowered teachers played key roles on administrative committees and had input into decision-making processes. "Teachers are professionals," Principal Weaver was fond of saying in support of his hands-off approach to leadership. So when Jeff learned that he would be accountable to each of the building principals, he hadn't given it much thought; he presumed that both Principal Weaver and Principal Malen would treat him like a professional.

As expected, Principal Weaver provided Jeff with ample space to develop the math lead role as he envisioned it. Jeff set to work creating a demonstration lesson schedule. He planned to visit each teacher's classroom once a month to model a lesson, followed by a debriefing session to help teachers reflect on their practice, problem-solve, and consider new teaching strategies. Jeff knew it would be challenging to model for all 24 teachers each month, but he had high standards for himself and was committed to strengthening teachers' math instruction. Before putting the plan in action, Jeff shared his idea with Principal Weaver, who replied, "You're the professional—you call the shots."

On the contrary, Principal Malen's definition of "professional" seemed to come from a different textbook entirely! On the very first day Principal Malen informed Jeff that they would be meeting biweekly to discuss his progress. She wanted him to participate in school activities, and she expected a monthly memo from him. Moreover, Principal Malen asked Jeff to suspend his goal of providing monthly demonstration lessons to all teachers. "Let's be a little more flexible with the time frame and with the kinds of interactions you have with the teachers. It may take a couple months for some folks to warm up to you. Others might prefer a different format for thinking about their instruction—maybe a math study group or something less intrusive." To Jeff's way of thinking, this was a "soft" approach that would enable teachers to avoid tough questions about their instruction.

Thinking back to that time, Jeff remembers how offended he was by Principal Malen's demands. He would be embarrassed to admit it now, but at the time he had referred to Principal Malen as a "micromanager on a power trip—one of those principals who has something to prove." He never would have imagined that Principal Malen's "micromanaging" would be the cornerstone of his success as the math lead at Portland Elementary.

Principal as Instructional Leader

Right from the start, and much to Jeff's dismay, Principal Malen seemed to want constant communication. She was continually leaving hand-scrawled Post-its stuck to his computer screen: "Jeff, stop by when you can—got an idea for math night!" or, "Jeff, have you read *Math Coach Field Guide*?" Jeff diligently responded to each of the notes, but in actuality he resented Principal Malen's directives and what he perceived as her presumptuous tone.

From what he could tell, Principal Malen didn't have anything better to do than ask him about math instruction, review math texts, dream up schoolwide math activities, and arrive unannounced at his door.

At the same time, Jeff appreciated the fact that Principal Malen was requiring all the teachers to work with him at least twice over the course of the year. In fact, she had mandated that teachers include "work with the math lead" as part of their yearly Professional Improvement Plan. And that wasn't all. Principal Malen informed the teachers that she would be paying close attention to math instruction when conducting evaluations. "I highly recommend that any teacher who feels uncertain about their math teaching should contact the math lead immediately. His job is to help you with instruction. Your job is to ask for help." Although this wasn't the kind of teacher professionalism that Jeff was accustomed to, he hoped the principal's directives would help get him into classrooms—especially since she had nixed his demonstration lesson schedule!

Before he knew it, Principal Malen had become an important source of information, ideas, and support for Jeff. His initial reluctance to involve Principal Malen in his work had evolved into a deep appreciation for the collaborative support she provided. Jeff could talk with her about his concerns and his accomplishments. She had even purchased two copies of *The Math Coach Field Guide: Charting Your Course* (Burns, Felux, & Snowdy, 2006) for them to read together and discuss in their regularly scheduled biweekly meeting.

Despite the openness of their relationship, Jeff was careful to guard the confidentiality of the teachers, never mentioning the names of individual teachers with whom he was working. In turn, Principal Malen did not ask him to reveal the names of "good" or "bad" teachers. Instead, she encouraged him to think positively about all the teachers and to capitalize on their strengths. "Let me be the source of pressure," she reminded him. "You are the source of support."

And, miraculously, he *had* become a source of support. It hadn't happened overnight, but by the end of the 1st year Jeff had interacted with all of the teachers at Portland Elementary. Half of them sought support above and beyond the mandated quota of two interactions. Then, in his 2nd year as the math lead, Jeff's work really began to take off. Nearly all the teachers at Portland Elementary requested his assistance beyond the mandated requirement. Teachers invited him to observe their instruction, the fourth-grade teachers initiated a pre-algebra study group, and the second-grade teachers were modeling for one another. Jeff continued to meet biweekly with Principal Malen. They were focusing their attention on interpreting the state test scores and helping teachers make sense of the results. Some of the resulting changes in classroom instruction had been profound.

Back at Westin . . .

Things at Westin weren't nearly so rosy. Although Principal Weaver continued to grant Jeff autonomy, Jeff was making little headway with the teachers. It quickly became clear that the modeling schedule was not going to work—even Jeff could see that it was too rigid—so, he had revised his approach. Taking his cue from the Portland teachers, Jeff worked to be more flexible and to meet teachers at their comfort level while simultaneously maintaining the focus on math. Contrary to the Portland teachers, Jeff's colleagues at Westin politely sidestepped nearly all of Jeff's efforts, even in his 2nd year as math lead. It seemed that the teachers were anti-modeling, antiteaming, anti-co-planning, anticonversation, or maybe antimath.

To make matters worse, Jeff had come to understand Principal Weaver's version of "autonomy" as a euphemism for neglect. Despite Jeff's repeated attempts to schedule discussion time with Principal Weaver, he had failed to arrange a single meaningful conversation about his work. In fact, Principal Weaver showed no interest in discussing math instruction or student achievement. When, after months of frustration, Jeff finally had a chance to voice his concerns, Principal Weaver replied, "I'm sure you'll figure it out—you're the professional."

Now, just hours before the board meeting, Jeff reflected on his initial misconceptions of both Principals Malen and Weaver. "How ironic," thought Jeff, "that the principal who most frequently describes teachers as empowered professionals has the most power over my future as the math lead teacher."

Open-Ended Case 4 Teaching Notes: Case Analysis

Activity. Case Analysis

Objective: To analyze the case using research on principal support for instructional teacher leadership. The analytical process will include three steps:

1. Establish the facts of the case.
2. Identify and define the problem.
3. Construct an appropriate response.

Each of these steps is elaborated below.

Step 1. Establishing the Facts of the Case

Begin by recalling the facts of the case using Table 2.1 in the Appendix as a guide. This process will help you establish what is known and unknown about the case. Be careful to distinguish between known facts and presumptions.

Further solidify your understanding of the case by comparing your list of facts with those of another classmate. Clarify and reconcile any areas of disagreement or inconsistency. When you feel confident that you know the facts of the case, proceed to Step 2.

Step 2. Identifying and Defining the Problem

The second step in analyzing the case is to identify and define the problem from the perspective of empirical research and/or theory. In this instance, you will examine the case from the perspective of research on principal support for instructional teacher leadership. To learn about this research, read the two articles indicated below and engage in the accompanying activities.

READING 1

Mangin, M. M. (2007). The role of elementary principals in teacher leadership initiatives. *Educational Administration Quarterly, 43*(3), 319–357.

This article describes the conditions that lead elementary principals to support the work of instructional teacher leaders. In particular, it explains how principals' knowledge of the position and their interaction with teacher leaders may facilitate support for teacher leadership.

This article is written in a highly technical style. To streamline the reading, we recommend some simple steps:

1. Begin with the abstract and introduction (pp. 319–320). This will help set the context for the article and let you know what to expect as a reader.
2. Skim through the literature review, methods, and study context sections (pp. 321–337). Just read the headings and subheadings. You may want to pause to look at Tables 1 and 2 in the article, which describe the participating schools/districts and the design of their teacher leader roles. Place a bookmark on Table 3 (p. 332), which you will consult when reading the study findings.
3. Carefully read the findings and summary/discussion on pages 338–352.

Part 1. On your own, write briefly about the following question:

How might the work of the instructional teacher leader be hindered or helped by the school principal?

Part 2. In small groups, share your written reflections from Part 1 above. Then work as a group to apply the findings from the article to Jeff's case to help you identify and define the problem he faces in his role as math lead.

1. Based on the findings presented in this article, how might you characterize the quality of support provided to Jeff by Principal Malen? If you were to include Principal Malen in Table 3 (see Mangin, 2007, p. 332), how would you categorize her knowledge of the math lead role and her interactions with Jeff? What evidence from the case would you use to support your decision?
2. Based on the findings presented in this article, how might you characterize the quality of support provided to Jeff by Principal Weaver? If you were to include Principal Weaver in Table 3 (see Mangin, 2007, p. 332), how would you categorize his knowledge of the math lead role and his interactions with Jeff? What evidence from the case would you use to support your decision?
3. Based on the findings presented in this article, what would Principal Weaver need to do to provide greater support to Jeff?
4. What steps might be taken by Jeff, Principal Weaver, Principal Malen, and/or district-level administrators to increase support for the math lead role?

READING 2

Pankake, A., & Moller, G. (2007). What the teacher leader needs from the principal. *Journal of Staff Development,* **28**(1), 32–36.

This article presents a set of eight strategies that principals can use to support the work of teacher leaders. These strategies include: 1) collaboratively building and monitoring an action plan, 2) negotiating the relationship, 3) being available, 4) providing access to human and fiscal resources, 5) maintaining the focus on instructional leadership, 6) helping to maintain balance to avoid overload, 7) protecting the coach's relationship with peers, and 8) providing leadership development opportunities. These strategies help create the necessary conditions for effective teacher leadership and promote collective leadership capacity.

Part 3. On your own, consider the ideas put forth in this article and their implications for instructional teacher leadership in general. Write briefly about the following question:

> How do these eight strategies combine to create a supportive environment for teacher leadership? What kinds of unsupportive conditions do they help reduce or eliminate?

Part 4. In small groups, share your written reflections from Part 3 above. Then work as a group to consider the relevance of the eight strategies to Jeff's case to help you delineate the challenges he faces with regard to principal support:

> To what extent are the eight support strategies evident in Jeff's work with Principals Malen and Weaver? Use Table 2.6 in the Appendix to help you systematically consider how each of the eight strategies is or is not evidenced. When you have completed the table, share your insights with a classmate. Pinpoint key areas where support is lacking and needs to be developed.

Step 3. Constructing an Appropriate Response

Next, you will construct an appropriate response to the challenges that Jeff faces using the concepts presented by Mangin (2007) and Pankake and Moller (2007). Through your response you will demonstrate your understanding of the ways in which principals can influence and support teacher leadership and how principal support can be mobilized. The question guiding your response is:

> What must happen for Jeff to receive the support necessary to be successful as the math lead teacher?

Part 1. In partners, outline a set of steps that need to be taken to increase the amount of support Jeff receives from Principal Weaver. Be clear about a) *what kinds* of supports are lacking, b) *how* the level of support will be increased, and c) *who* will need to take action to increase support for Jeff's work.

Part 2. On your own, deepen your understanding of principal support for teacher leadership by examining vignette number 7, "*Work with the Principal: Lucy,*" from the first part of this volume (Vignettes 5 and 8 about Cassie and Abby also address issues of principal support). Analyze the vignette for evidence of principal support as well as lack of support. In your analysis, use the concepts presented by Mangin (2007) and Pankake and Moller (2007) to help you interpret the vignette and devise a response. Outline your response in a short memo.

Additional Reading Sources

To learn more about principal support for teacher leadership, we recommend the following:

Blase, J., & Blase, J. (1998). *Handbook of instructional leadership: How really good principals promote teaching and learning.* Thousand Oaks, CA: Corwin Press.

Drago-Severson, E., & Pinto, K. (2004). From barriers to breakthroughs: Principals' strategies for overcoming challenges to teachers' transformational learning. *The Journal of School Leadership, 14,* 653–685.

Marks, H. M., & Printy, S. M. (2003). Principal leadership & school performance: An integration of transformational & instructional leadership. *Educational Administration Quarterly, 39*(3), 370–397.

Moller, G., & Pankake, A. (2006). *Lead with me: A principal's guide to teacher leadership.* Larchmont, NY: Eye on Education.

Printy, S. M. (2008). Leadership for teacher learning: A community of practice perspective. *Educational Administration Quarterly, 44*(2), 187–226.

Smylie, M. A., & Brownlee-Conyers, J. (1992). Teacher leaders and their principals: Exploring the development of new working relationships. *Educational Administration Quarterly, 28*(2), 150–184.

Open-Ended Case 5.
Data-Based Improvement: Janie

This case introduces the challenge of using data to promote instructional improvement. Janie worked as the literacy coach at Blackstone Elementary, a K–5 school in a large urban district. Blackstone had 95% African American students with a small Latino population. All of the students were low-income. In this case, Janie struggled to improve teacher implementation of new literacy practices and to convince teachers to deepen their use of data to inform instruction. After reading and establishing the facts of the case, research on data usage will be used to interpret the case and promote the identification of a set of strategies for addressing the dilemmas Janie faces in her work.

Getting Started

Janie had been a third-grade teacher at Blackstone Elementary School for 3 years when she was selected to be the literacy coach. The promotion came as a surprise to her, since there were many teachers who were senior to her in the school, but she was thrilled with the opportunity. "I consider Janie to be our best Language Arts teacher, our most innovative teacher and a natural leader," Janie's principal stated. "I knew she was the right person for the job and wasn't going to let her relative newness to teaching deter me from appointing her."

Blackstone Elementary School worked in partnership with a local university, their "university literacy partner." The university partner created the literacy program that the school adopted, and a key component of Janie's job was to support teachers' implementation of the program. Janie's efforts were supported by a university literacy mentor who met regularly with Janie to monitor and guide her progress.

In her 1st year as the literacy coach, Janie's approach to supporting the teachers had been to provide monthly whole-group staff development sessions focused on the literacy framework developed by the literacy partner. Each month Janie presented a single practice, such as literature circles or read-alouds, and asked teachers to focus on that literacy practice for the month following. At the next staff development session, the teachers would debrief about how the practice worked in their classroom and then Janie would introduce a new practice. This model of literacy coaching—introducing a practice and having teachers try it—came largely from the school's university partner.

Janie used this same approach in grade-level meetings. She introduced a new practice that was grade-specific and gave teachers an opportunity to ask questions and discuss the practice. Then the teachers tried the activity in their classrooms. At the next grade-level meeting teachers had a chance to share how the practice had worked in their classrooms. Initially, Janie was pleased with this use of her time and was enthusiastic about the teachers' receptiveness to her work.

After a year of using the whole-group and grade-level staff development approach, Janie became more and more uncertain about its effectiveness. Teachers rarely shared their experiences implementing the literacy practices, and Janie wondered if anyone was actually using them. Not being in classrooms, Janie had no idea if teachers were implementing the new practices or the extent to which instruction was actually changing. Janie began to think about her role in an entirely different way, wondering if she needed to spend time in classrooms with teachers.

At the same time, Janie was surprised to discover a sense of complacency that was due to the faculty's perception of the school as outside the threat of intervention.

The literacy partner had an additional concern about the progress being made at Blackstone, which Sadie Williams, the university literacy mentor, expressed to Janie in a meeting at the end of her 1st year as literacy coach. "It is about the formative assessments that go with the literacy materials," Sadie stated to Janie. "Are the teachers using them to inform their literacy instruction?" Janie shook her head. "I honestly don't know," she responded. The two stayed silent for a moment. "Don't worry, Janie," Sadie stated with her hand on Janie's shoulder. "Let's start working on how we can improve for next year."

Digging Deeper

It was the beginning of Janie's 2nd year as literacy coach. At the first faculty meeting of the year, she announced to teachers and the administration the new plan that she and Sadie had developed. "This year we will have two changes in our approach to implementing the literacy framework," she announced. The first change, she told the teachers, would be that she would observe in classrooms and co-teach. She provided the teachers with a schedule of classroom visits throughout the year. "We will continue to have grade-level professional development, like last year," she explained in the meeting. "The second change in focus will be that we will largely use the grade-level meeting time to work with the formative assessment data you are collecting, to improve and differentiate instruction." Janie distributed a page with the topics of focus for the grade-level meetings. "This year we will take the next step, where I will come and observe you implementing the practices we discuss. It is time to dig a little deeper."

The following Tuesday, the third-grade teachers at Blackstone had their first meeting about using the formative assessments that went with the literacy framework. "Today we are going to discuss using the formative assessments to differentiate instruction," Janie explained. She handed out an overview of the literacy framework with a list of the assessment tools that connected to each literacy practice. "Now we are going to examine the student work that you brought with you. We will use this rubric to determine what the students know and what they still need to learn in relation to reading comprehension." Pairs of teachers worked together to sort their student work into groups using the rubric. The conversation lasted an hour. Janie left the meeting feeling energized. She scheduled observations in the third-grade teachers' classrooms for the days that followed.

A week later Janie sat in the back of Mrs. Talia's third-grade classroom, observing a literacy lesson. Mrs. Talia opened the 90-minute literacy block with a read-aloud. She asked her third-graders to gather on the reading rug in the corner. Mrs. Talia sat in a white rocking chair, and the students gathered at her feet. She pulled out a large print book and began to read to the students. When she finished reading, Mrs. Talia put down the book and explained, "Now that we have read together, we are going to work on answering some questions about the book. Please return to your seats."

The students returned to their desks. Mrs. Talia handed out a worksheet. "Let's start with question one. In the story, what is Susan's problem?" Janie continued to sit in the back of the room, shocked at what she was observing. What happened to the small-group discussions that were supposed to follow the read-aloud? Would this whole-group worksheet activity continue for the entire block? Once the students had settled into individually completing the worksheet, Janie approached Mrs. Talia and motioned to join her in the hallway. "What happened to the small-group activity?" Janie asked. Mrs. Talia looked at the floor for a moment before responding, "This activity just seems more important given the requirements for the district standardized tests," she responded, shifting from one foot to the other. "The literacy program has a lot of nice things for students to do, and they like it, but it seems more like extras than the basics that they need." Mrs. Talia explained that she used the literacy activities that Janie introduced as a supplement, when she had "extra time." "What about differentiating instruction based on the formative assessments, like we talked about in the grade-level meeting," Janie asked. "I guess I feel like if all students need to do well on the third-grade test, they need to be taught at the third-grade level," Mrs. Talia said.

Janie's shock deepened as she visited more classrooms. While teachers welcomed her into their classrooms, she discovered that Mrs. Talia's approach was the rule rather than the exception. Teachers were only partially implementing literacy framework activities. And while they were willing to discuss formative assessment, analyzing student work, and differentiating instruction at grade-level meetings, they were not taking the next steps in their classroom to act upon the results of the assessments. Upset and uncertain, she called Sadie Williams, her university literacy mentor, to discuss her concerns. "What I see in classrooms are bits and pieces of the practices, jumbled and incomplete," she told Sadie. "The teachers are not applying what they learn in the grade-level meetings about assessment." She told Sadie that while she observed partial components of the literacy practices in most classrooms, only small changes seemed to be occurring in teachers' practice. "How do teachers respond to your questions and suggestions?" Sadie asked Janie. "They certainly smile and are pleasant enough when I offer advice," Janie said. "But when I come back the next time, my suggestions are generally not being implemented." Janie and Sadie discussed a variety of approaches to encourage teachers to make changes in their practice and to assist them in incorporating the assessment results.

When Deeper Isn't Deep Enough

Janie perceived that she worked in a school that had great strengths. Teachers worked together voluntarily and professionally. Teachers were positive about the school and about their work with students. The school was relatively small, and staff members had developed strong relationships of trust. Teachers attended the workshops Sadie provided on literacy instruction and generally seemed receptive to new ideas. "But practice isn't changing," Janie stated in a meeting with Sadie. "We are here in this wonderful school, and we are all happy. But are we happy because we are complacent?" she wondered. She further explained:

> Sometimes the teachers here, and even administrators, talk about Blackstone like we are a high-achieving school. I want to give them a wake-up call and say, Okay, almost *half* of our students are still not at grade level or average achievement on standardized tests. How can we be so satisfied with that? How can our expectations for our students be that low? I fear sometimes that it is far too easy to feel

like we are doing well only because we are in a [school] system where some schools are doing so poorly.

Janie and Sadie discussed the standardized test scores for Blackstone. "This is another problem," Janie stated. "Teachers see the standardized tests as requiring different skills from the ones instilled by the literacy framework. They think they need to give their students basic skills to do well on the standardized tests. They think the skills developed using the literacy framework are fun but unnecessary."

As the 2nd year of her work as literacy coach came to a close, Janie continued her workshops and observations. She patiently offered advice to teachers on how to improve their implementation of the literacy practices. She continued to meet with teachers about the ways to think about assessing what students know and what they still need to learn. At the final meeting with the university literacy partner staff, Janie openly expressed her frustration. "I feel like I am saying the same things over and over. Will it get through to them? I feel like I am stuck." In response, the literacy partner staff provided suggestions and comments. "Deepening this work, pushing the teachers to think more critically about their instruction using data, is essential to our success," Sadie stated. The leader of the literacy partnership agreed, "We can't continue this way, with practices half-implemented."

The meeting ended and the staff from the literacy partner organization departed. It was clear that they were beginning to get impatient with teachers' lack of progress implementing the literacy practices. Principal Bailey and Janie stayed to talk more after the partners left. "They want to know, and rightfully so, why teachers talk the talk but don't walk the walk," Janie remarked to Principal Bailey. "All I keep saying is, I don't know. I don't know why they don't."

As Janie thought ahead to the coming year, she wondered how to proceed. The school's small size allowed her time to visit every teacher regularly. Grade-level meeting structures were in place, with time set aside for planning, collaborating, and professional development. The positive school culture at Blackstone meant that teachers were generally willing to allow her into their classrooms to observe practice. Teachers were open to talking about assessing students and differentiating instruction. But practice did not seem to be changing. How could she convince teachers to implement these practices more deeply without damaging relationships of trust she had built? How could she work with teachers to deepen their understanding of student assessment? "I kept telling the teachers this year that we are digging deeper, digging deeper, digging deeper," she stated to Principal Bailey. "What do you do when 'deeper' isn't deep enough?"

Open-Ended Case 5 Teaching Notes: Case Analysis

ACTIVITY. CASE ANALYSIS

Objective: To analyze the case using theories of data-based improvement and scaling up reform. The analytical process will include three steps:

1. Establish the facts of the case.
2. Identify and define the problem.
3. Construct an appropriate response.

Each of these steps is elaborated below.

Step 1. Establishing the Facts of the Case

Begin by recalling the facts of the case using Table 2.1 in the Appendix as a guide. This process will help you establish what is known and unknown about the case. Be careful to distinguish between known facts and presumptions.

Further solidify your understanding of the case by comparing your list of facts with those of another classmate. Clarify and reconcile any areas of disagreement or inconsistency. When you feel confident that you know the facts of the case, proceed to Step 2.

Step 2. Identifying and Defining the Problem

The second step in analyzing the case of Blackstone Elementary is to identify and define the problem. In the analysis of this case you will draw upon the analytical lens of *data usage in education*. Read the highlighted articles below and complete the activities described below.

READING 1

Boudett, K. P., City, E. A., & Murnane, R. J. (2006). The "Data Wise" improvement process: Eight steps for using test data to improve teaching and learning. *Harvard Education Letter, 22*(1), 1–3.

Boudett and colleagues highlight eight steps in the "Data Wise" improvement process to assist schools in preparing, inquiring, and acting to improve data usage. These steps include: 1) organizing for collaborative work, 2) building assessment literacy, 3) creating data overview, 4) digging into student data, 5) examining instruction, 6) developing an action plan,

7) preparing a plan to assess progress, and 8) acting and assessing. These strategies help to create the necessary conditions for effective teacher leadership and promote collective leadership capacity.

Part 1. On your own or with a partner:

1. Evaluate the organizational capacity for data usage at Blackstone Elementary using Table 2.7 in the Appendix as a guide. Assess Blackstone's existing resources, strengths, and weaknesses on each of the eight steps Boudett et al. identify for using data to improve teaching and learning.
2. As Janie, write a short memo (2–3 pages) to Blackstone's principal, Principal Bailey, summarizing the school's organizational readiness for data usage. Draw upon your summary and assessment in Table 2.7.

READING 2

Schmoker, M. (2003). First things first: Demystifying data analysis. *Educational Leadership*, 60(5), 22–24.

In "Demystifying Data Analysis," Schmoker stresses researchers' "tendency to complicate the use and analysis of student achievement data." "The effective use of data," Schmoker states, "depends on simplicity and economy." Schmoker emphasizes the importance of simplifying the use of data through focused data usage and goal setting.

Part 2. In small groups, generate a list of the possible data sources that might be used to promote improvement in instructional practice at Blackstone. Begin by making a list of data sources identified in the case. Then, add a list of potential data sources that Blackstone leaders might gather using what you have learned from Schmoker.

Step 3. Constructing an Appropriate Response

Next you will construct an appropriate response to the challenges that Janie faces using the concepts presented by Boudett et al. (2006) and Schmoker (2003). Through your response you will demonstrate your understanding of the role that data play in instructional teacher leaders' promotion of instructional improvement

Part 1. In your small group, role-play as a grade-level team at Blackstone Elementary. Identify grade level goals. Advocate for various goals and data sources, identifying the strengths, weaknesses, and tradeoffs of different goals and data.

Part 2. Imagine that you are Janie and write a memo to Sadie Williams and Principal Bailey outlining your work plan for the coming year. In this short memo (1–2 pages), articulate the ways in which you will work with teachers and data to improve instructional practice in literacy.

Additional Reading Sources

To learn more about data-based improvement, we recommend the following:

Copland, M. (2003). Leadership of inquiry: Building and sustaining capacity for school improvement. *Educational Evaluation and Policy Analysis, 25*, 375–395.

Halverson, R., Grigg, J., Prichett, R., & Thomas, C. (2005). *The new instructional leadership: Creating data-driven instructional systems in schools.* WCER Working Paper 2005-9, Wisconsin Center for Education Research, University of Wisconsin–Madison.

Lachat, M., & Smith. S. (2005). Practices that support data use in urban schools. *Journal of Education for Students Placed at Risk, 10*(3), 333–349.

McLaughlin, M., & Mitra, D. (2003). *The cycle of inquiry as the engine of school reform: Lessons from the Bay Area School Reform Collaborative.* Report, Center for Research on the Context of Teaching, Stanford University, Stanford, CA.

Popham, W. J., Cruse, K. L., Rankin, S. C., Sandifer, P. D., & Williams, P. L. (1985). Measurement-driven instruction: It's on the road. *Phi Delta Kappan, 66*, 628–634.

Young, V. M. (2006). Teachers' use of data: Loose coupling, agenda setting, and team norms. *American Journal of Education, 112*, 521–548.

Part 3

Situating Instructional Teacher Leadership in Complex Contexts: Scaffolded Case Studies

The third part of this volume contains three scaffolded case studies that explore instructional teacher leadership in complex school environments. Each case is structured to unfold in three sections, allowing for incremental analysis as more information is revealed and the case becomes more complex. The cases portray the contexts within which teacher leaders work, with each case offering a different perspective on contextual influences.

In addition, the three scaffolded cases are layered differently to reveal a variety of influential contexts. The case of Barley School begins with the school and neighborhood contexts. Layered upon these contextual descriptions is a depiction of the literacy reform undertaken in the school. The third section of the case focuses on the literacy facilitator role.

The case of the Sexton School District begins with a description of the district context. Layered upon this is a description of the Comprehensive School Reform model adopted by the district. The final section of the case situates the math coach role within the context of district-level professional development intended to support school-level reform.

The case of Aurora Elementary is organized to consider the reform initiative and the work of the instructional teacher leader from the perspectives of different school staff members. The case unfolds chronologically to tell the story of the implementation of a literacy reform. As the story unfolds it is told through four different lenses: the principal, the school literacy coach, the regional literacy coach, and a classroom teacher.

Each scaffolded case is followed by a set of teaching notes, which include new analytical lenses for interpreting the cases, suggested readings, and activities. Engagement with scaffolded case studies that unfold over time and within the context of complex environments can deepen understanding of instructional teacher leadership and the challenge of effective implementation.

Barley School

In this section of the case, you will read about the context of Barley School, including the neighborhood, students, teachers, principal, culture, policies, and politics. This contextual information will provide a foundation for learning about the work of the literacy facilitator.

A Changing Context

Barley School is a K–8 elementary school located in the West Alton neighborhood of a large city. The West Alton neighborhood has experienced a great deal of change over the past 20 to 30 years. Once a vibrant area with a large number of African American–owned businesses and a vibrant street life, the neighborhood has transformed into empty storefronts, graffiti-covered walls, and trash-strewn streets. Between 1980 and 1995, the neighborhood population decreased by more than 40%, leaving housing vacant and streets empty. On the street where Barley School is located, there was once a bookstore, a grocery store, a YMCA, a pharmacy, and several small barber operations. By the mid-1990s, only the YMCA and the school remained open, with the remaining businesses boarded up and abandoned. One longtime resident of the West Alton neighborhood described the changes he had witnessed over the years:

> I remember the time when every café was filled, when every business was booming, when the streets were clean and the parks were new and full of kids. Now all that is left are the taverns, which are overflowing with poor Black folks. It is as though when the businesses left, they took with them not just the money but the energy and the sense of purpose and hope.

Some of the changes in the neighborhood are mirrored in the students attending Barley School, who have become increasingly impoverished. The percentage of students receiving free or reduced-price lunch increased from just over half in the early 1980s to 100% in 1994. The perception of Barley School's teachers is that the students come from more difficult circumstances and thus also have more social and emotional needs. One teacher stated:

> The students have challenges that are different from before. They have drug houses next door. They have parents on drugs. They mostly live with a single parent. Some have health issues. All of that influences our work as teachers.

As the neighborhood has changed and the student population has shifted, so have the teachers who work in the school. In the 1970s, Barley School primarily was staffed by teachers who lived in the area around the school. Many of them walked to work and knew the families of the students in their classrooms. Barley School was, in that respect, truly a neighborhood school. By 1995 none of the teachers in the school lived in the neighborhood. Many commuted long distances from the north side of the city to work at Barley School. In addition, school leaders perceived that they had a more difficult time filling empty teacher positions. The assistant principal described the challenges of teacher hiring. "We have the problem of drive-bys," she stated. "Prospective teacher candidates drive by the school and once they see where it is, no way will they apply."

A New Leader and a Culture of Mistrust

Eleanor Stillman has been the principal at Barley School for 7 years. Prior to being hired as the principal, Stillman was a fourth-grade teacher and then assistant principal at Giles Elementary, a school a few miles west of Barley School. She had spent her entire 14-year career at Giles and left to take the principalship at Barley School only because she wanted to be a principal and the position was unlikely to open anytime soon at Giles. "I had a very good relationship with the principal at Giles. We worked very well together. He was the one who suggested I would be a good principal and that I should spread my wings," Stillman told the hiring committee when she interviewed at Barley School.

Barley School has 28 teachers. There are three classrooms each for grades 1 through 8 and four kindergarten classrooms. When Principal Stillman arrived, Barley School had 700 students in a building that could hold more than 1,000. Due to the decline in overall student population, classrooms sit empty in the building and several are used as storage areas. "We are what the district calls an 'underutilized' school," one teacher explained. "It means we have a lot fewer students than the capacity of the building."

The faculty is a mix of very seasoned and very inexperienced teachers, with few who fall in between. Twenty of the teachers have been at the school for more than 15 years. Eight of the teachers have been at the school for less than 5. This division between newer and more experienced teachers also falls along grade-level lines, with the newer teachers staffing classrooms between kindergarten and fourth grade and the more experienced teachers working in fifth through eighth grades.

Principal Stillman arrived to find that low levels of trust permeated relationships among teachers. Part of the foundation for this lack of trust fell along the experience rift. The more experienced teachers perceived the younger teachers as trying to change the school in ways that might alter the fundamental character of the school. At the same time, the newer teachers thought the more experienced teachers were teaching in a traditional manner that needed updating. The divide along grade-level lines exacerbated the difficulty of the situation. The senior teachers in the higher grade levels felt that the junior teachers' ideas were only appropriate for "little kids." In the words of one seventh-grade teacher who has taught for 23 years, "I don't see learning centers being appropriate for the kids in my class. Let them do that downstairs in primary."

Another complexity to the situation was that many of the younger lower-grade teachers are White while the more experienced upper-grade teachers are African American. "Things are seen as racial that I don't think are racial," one White teacher stated. On the flip side, an African American teacher noted, "They don't understand Black culture, that is the problem."

Parent–administration relationships were similarly complex. Principal Stillman replaced a principal who had been at the school for 20 years. When Principal Evans retired, many of the teachers at Barley School were crushed. "Principal Evans was our father figure. He was our grandfather. The kids loved him. We loved him," one seventh-grade teacher explained. Teachers were more loyal to Principal Evans than parents. While parents liked Principal Evans as a person, they were skeptical at times of his ability to run the school. "He was a good father figure to the kids," one parent explained. "But he let the teachers run wild, scream at the kids, do whatever they damn well pleased." The arrival of Principal Stillman seemed to be marked with cautious optimism. "Can't get any worse," one parent responded when asked what she thought would happen to the school with the new principal's arrival.

Parent–teacher relationships prior to Stillman's arrival were strained. Parents often walked into classrooms to confront teachers about the treatment or instruction their children were receiving. Several times, conflicts between teachers and parents escalated to the point that the police were called. "For a long time, we have been fighting with parents here," one fifth-grade teacher explained. "It hasn't been a positive situation with parents at all," stated a third-grade teacher.

Principal Stillman realized upon arrival that the challenges she faced as principal were significant. "The children in this school have needs. The relationships are strained. The instruction needs work. Where do I even begin?"

Building a Foundation for Change

Upon her arrival as principal, Principal Stillman focused on what she perceived to be the "basic school functioning." When asked what her top priority was upon arrival, she stated that it was safety:

> There are a lot of things going on in this school that risk the welfare of our students, staff, and parents. It is out of control. Parents just walk in and out and scream at teachers during the school day. Students and teachers are screaming at each other. Students are getting kicked out of class and there are regularly twenty kids in the office for me or the assistant principal to deal with. We need order. Plain and simple. That has to come before I can even think about instructional practice.

Principal Stillman didn't waste any time making changes in the school. Within her first few weeks as principal, it was clear that she intended to push for change in the school right away. Principal Stillman instituted four policy changes related to room assignments, discipline, visitor management, and school governance.

With regard to room assignments, the teachers returned to school in the fall to find that Principal Stillman had reassigned rooms. Teachers who had been in the same room for more than a decade were relocated. "Teachers were assigned rooms based on favoritism and seniority rather than based on what was best for kids and the school," Principal Stillman explained. In the new arrangement, grade-level teachers were placed in clusters together and the older children were placed on the upper floors, separated from the younger children. For the more senior teachers who were assigned the higher grade levels, this meant the unpopular walk up the stairs to the third and fourth floors of the building. "It took me a long time to get my room, Room One-eleven," Ms. Stiles, a seventh-grade teacher explained. "It was right there, next to the entrance, near the office, near everything. Now I have to walk all the way up to the fourth floor. I am upset."

The second major policy change focused on student behavior. In going over the files, Principal Evans saw stacks of parent complaints about students being removed from class unfairly. During the interview process, she also heard a lot about this from the parents on the hiring committee. Principal Stillman thought that addressing parent complaints was a key part of building better relationships with parents. As a result, she instituted a new discipline policy for students. It involved a warning followed by a system of checks on the chalkboard before sending the students to the disciplinarian. From Principal Stillman's perspective, this discipline policy would make the treatment of student infractions uniform from classroom to classroom. Teachers had mixed responses to the policy. "In some ways, it felt like she was saying I don't know how to handle my kids," one sixth-grade teacher stated. "I was offended, like it seemed like I was being reprimanded to be given such a policy," another teacher said. Other teachers felt it was a positive development, "I think it will keep things more consistent, that is important," a second-grade teacher stated.

Principal Stillman's third change in policy was welcomed by the teachers. The principal immediately instituted a "no classroom disruptions" policy and hired a security guard to manage all visitors to the building. Parents who came into the building had to sign in and make appointments to talk with teachers about their children. The principal or assistant principal was always to be present as a mediator for such meetings. "When I read the new policy limiting visitors, I breathed a sigh of relief," one teacher stated. "I thought to myself, finally I can teach in peace," stated another.

Principal Stillman's final policy change was intended to lay the foundation for teacher involvement in school governance. She created a nine-person Leadership Council. She and the assistant principal would serve on the council as well as the counselor, the social worker, a special education teacher, and four teachers. This council would oversee the school improvement planning process mandated by the school system. In the first year, Principal Stillman had to push several teachers to join. "Two of the positions teachers volunteered for, the rest I had to prod and push." Teacher leadership in the building was very limited, and Stillman perceived that instituting teacher involvement in governance was going to involve "a major paradigm shift for most faculty members of what it means to be a teacher."

The arrival of Principal Stillman marked a new era at Barley School, one that teachers in the school entered with mixed feelings. She focused her energies on school order and functioning and on increasing safety and improving relationships. At the end of her 2nd year as principal, Ms. Stillman felt that she had made some progress in building a foundation for improved instruction. "I see the school as being at a different place in terms of culture. But I have not even touched the heart of the school: teaching and learning." In the days that followed, Principal Stillman would begin the long journey of improving instructional practice at the school.

PART TWO: INTRODUCING THE LITERACY REFORM

In this section of the case, you will read about the literacy reform under-
taken by Barley School. You will learn about the theoretical underpin-
nings of the literacy approach and the selection and training of the literacy
facilitator.

Targeting Instructional Practice

In her 3rd year as principal, Principal Stillman wanted to continue to make
the school safer for all involved and to create stronger relationships of trust
among teachers, teachers and the administrators, and the school and parents. But she also planned to incorporate a new focus: instructional practice.

As the school year began, Principal Stillman began to spend more time
in classrooms observing teachers. She was largely shocked by what she saw.
The lack of coherence across classrooms, even in the same grade level, was
obvious. At the seventh-grade level, for example, one teacher was using a
reading text for fifth-graders. Another was using the seventh-grade text from
a different publisher. The format was equally mixed. Teachers in some classrooms were using worksheets and students sat in rows. In other classrooms,
students were working in small groups, engaging in discussion, and present-
ing their work.

Given the incoherence of both instructional materials and priorities,
Principal Stillman decided that the top priority had to be finding a set of
instructional materials that all teachers would use.

While Stillman was in the process of looking for the right instructional
intervention, she attended a meeting at the district central office. A presentation was made about available funding for schools to work in networks
with external partners. Time was given at the meeting for principals to meet
one another and to meet potential partner organizations. Groups of principals would then apply together with the partner as a network to work together to improve their schools.

The reform focused on bringing together networks of schools that would
work with an external partner that would work with the schools to improve.
Each partnership was different. For example, one partner focused on overall school climate, one on improving math instruction, another on improving student self-esteem. The partners were also very different. Some were
university-based, while others were corporate school improvement organizations or unions.

Immediately, Principal Stillman knew she had two goals in finding a
network of schools and a partner organization. First, she knew that she
wanted to work on improving literacy instruction because she felt literacy

was foundational for improvement in other subjects. Second, she also knew that she wanted to be in a network with schools that were similar to her own. Specifically, she wanted to find principals of schools that were located in neighborhoods that were like West Alton and that served impoverished African American students. "I went in very focused on what I wanted to improve and who I wanted to do it with," Principal Stillman stated.

Principal Stillman found such a network and partner. The group of schools called themselves the Network for School Improvement and applied to work with the Leadership and Literacy Improvement Center (LLIC), a local school reform research organization.

The Literacy Program and Partner

The Network for School Improvement was organized by the Leadership and Literacy Improvement Center (LLIC), which was a school reform research organization. LLIC was one of several organizations that were instrumental in the passing of a major piece of reform legislation in the city. Over the years the organization expanded from its role as a community organizer to providing services to help schools improve. LLIC's approach was based on the philosophy of community organizing, helping individuals develop capacity as leaders to advocate for themselves. Within that framework, LLIC had four major goals:

1. Identify and develop strong leaders. LLIC's logic was that expanding leadership beyond the principal was essential to school improvement. In addition, the organization leaders believed that collaboration within high-functioning teams would build strong leadership. To promote these two leadership goals, LLIC worked to assist principals in the identification of other potentially strong and effective leaders in their schools, including an internal candidate for a literacy facilitator position. This person would work as a coach and mentor for other teachers. Then, after the literacy facilitator was established, the organization worked to help the Barley School build teacher teams to engage in instructional improvement work in literacy.

2. Promoting the use of "best practices" in literacy. LLIC published a 50-page guide to promising practices in literacy development. The resource guide contained descriptions of specific "best practices." That would promote improvements in literacy instruction. LLIC did not believe in a prescriptive or scripted approach to instructional improvement. Rather, the logic was that if teachers were given better tools from which to choose, they could improve their instruction with the support of the literacy facilitator and the teacher teams.

3. Develop and consolidate teacher collaboration. LLIC's philosophy was that collaboration among teachers was essential to increase coherence, deepen teacher thinking about instructional practice, and promote improvement across classrooms.

4. Broaden assessment practices and intervention strategies. Another cornerstone of LLIC's work was to promote the creation, implementation, and use of locally developed formative and summative assessments. LLIC leaders argued that learning more about what students know and don't know was an important part of targeting areas for improvement, both for students, and for teachers to improve their practice.

LLIC worked with Barley School in a variety of ways to support these four goals. Literacy experts on LLIC's staff worked closely with the literacy facilitator. This included helping the literacy facilitator learn the best practices in literacy and design effective professional development for teachers. The literacy facilitator role was not prescribed by LLIC; rather, the LLIC staff worked with each school to define an appropriate role based on school culture and needs. LLIC staff members also provided support in the development of the formative and summative assessments at the school. Assessment experts on the staff worked with the literacy facilitator and the teachers in the process of developing assessments.

The Selection and Training of the Literacy Facilitator

Kimberly Adams was a third-grade teacher at Barley School for 3 years when Principal Stillman called her into her office and asked her to be the literacy facilitator. It was a warm spring day near the end of the school year. The invitation was a shock to Kimberly. As one of the more junior teachers at the school, she wasn't sure how she would be received in a leadership role. "You have been on the Leadership Council since your first year, you are among our best teachers in literacy, you have the potential to do great things," Principal Stillman told Kimberly. "I am not sure anyone will ever listen to me," Kimberly responded. "This is a journey we will take together, one day at a time, what do you say?" Principal Stillman responded. Kimberly agreed to take on the role.

Kimberly began her role by engaging in intensive summer training with the five other literacy facilitators from the five other network schools in the Network for School Improvement. LLIC sent the new facilitators to a literacy learning workshop in Atlanta. The workshop considered a set of best practices in literacy. For a week in the heat of Atlanta in July, Kimberly listened to experts talk about literature circles, writer's workshop, guided reading, and guided writing. She watched videos of children reading and learned assessment frameworks to think about what a student knew and still needed to learn in reading and writing. She talked with other teachers, as well as with her fellow network literacy facilitators, about what she was learning. It was an exhilarating time for Kimberly. "I feel so renewed, I learned so many new ideas," Kimberly told Principal Stillman. "I have so many exciting ideas, I can't wait to share them."

Kimberly then returned home to another set of meetings with LLIC and the network literacy facilitators. Together, the literacy experts from LLIC and the literacy facilitators worked to devise a strategy and schedule for their 1st year of work. They decided to focus on five best practices in literacy by grade level. They would present the practices in professional development workshops that the teachers from all five schools would attend. Having these workshops as a network would cut down on the amount of preparation for each literacy facilitator, since each would serve as the lead for one of the workshops for the network of schools. Each would become an "expert" in one practice. At the same time, they would be able to deepen their knowledge of the other four practices by attending and assisting with the workshops led by the other network literacy facilitators. "It was the best of all worlds for all of us," Kimberly explained. "The network concept really expanded our knowledge base and decreased our workload."

Following each workshop, each literacy facilitator would return to her school to model the practice in one teacher's classroom in a grade level while the other teachers came to watch. Network funding would be used to provide substitutes for teacher's classrooms while they were observing the demonstration lesson in a peer's classroom. Then the literacy facilitator would follow up with teachers at the grade level, observing them trying the practice in their own classroom and co-teaching as needed.

Kimberly spent the rest of her summer working on her own to fill in the details of her schedule for the coming year. Kimberly decided that she would pair grade levels for these demonstration lessons. First and second grades, third and fourth grades, fifth and sixth grades, and seventh and eighth grades would be combined to observe demonstration lessons. She made a list of the 28 teachers at Barley School and worked out a preliminary schedule of a demonstration lesson for the paired grade levels that followed the workshop series for those grades. She made a schedule for the observations and follow-up in each teacher's classroom. It was an ambitious schedule, but she felt ready to face her first day of her new job.

PART THREE: A TALE OF THREE CHALLENGES

In this section of the case, you will read about the implementation process of the literacy initiative. In particular, you will read about three challenges faced by the principal and the literacy facilitator and the approaches taken to manage those challenges.

Building a Foundation for Change

It was the 1st day of school and Kimberly was nervous but excited. "How are you?" Principal Stillman asked as Kimberly entered the building. "I am as nervous as I was on my first day of teaching," Kimberly admitted. "I hardly slept last night and I had way too much coffee this morning!" she added, shaking her head. Principal Stillman laughed and put her hand on Kimberly's shoulder. "You are going to do great!"

Kimberly and Principal Stillman had no idea that the first of three critical challenges to the literacy initiative and the work of the literacy facilitator would be defined on that very first day: the challenge of bringing together a staff divided.

Challenge 1: Bridging a Cultural Divide

The teachers piled into the library for the first staff meeting of the school year. It was the 2nd day of school. Spirits were high and chatter was loud as teachers caught up on stories of summer vacations while they settled into the chairs. The clatter subsided somewhat as Principal Stillman walked into the library. "Good morning, everyone," she nodded. She handed around the agenda for the meeting. Whispered chatter and quiet laughter continued as teachers finished up their stories and handed around the agendas. The quiet din turned to shocked silence as the teachers read through the agenda. "We are doing WORK today?" a fifth-grade teacher stage-whispered. Principal Stillman smiled. "Indeed, we are doing some work this morning," she responded to the whisperer. "This is a big year. This is the year we turn literacy instruction around in our school." As she made this last statement, she motioned to Kimberly to stand. "I would like to introduce to you our new literacy facilitator, Kimberly Adams." There were several audible gasps and open mouths throughout the library.

Kimberly had not imagined this moment happening in quite this way, although she was not surprised. The gasps she heard mirrored her own shock at the end of the previous school year when Principal Stillman had asked her to be the literacy facilitator. "Kimberly is going to talk today about the literacy initiative in which we are now engaged. Kimberly?"

Kimberly walked to the front of the library, her legs shaking a bit as she walked. She handed out the binders she had prepared for each teacher, which contained the schedule of the network professional development sessions, the demonstration lessons for the grade-level pairs, and the scheduled follow-up sessions that would take place in each teacher's classroom. Also included was the short description of each of the literacy best practices that would be the focus of the demonstration lessons and the professional development sessions throughout the year. There were some pages that described LLIC and the literacy partner's goals and foci. Finally, there were a few pages that described Kimberly's role as literacy facilitator. "Let's walk through it together, shall we?" Kimberly said to the teachers. "Open your binders to the first page." As she looked out at the teachers she suddenly noticed that all the young, lower-grades teachers sat on the right side of the room and all the more experienced, middle- and upper-grades teachers sat on the left side of the room. It was a realization that would come to her mind again many times in the year that followed.

A week later, Kimberly stood in a seventh-grade classroom, ready to do a demonstration lesson for the seventh- and eighth-grade teachers on writer's workshop. Five of the six teachers had substitute teachers in their classrooms so they could observe the demonstration. The sixth teacher's classroom was the location of the demonstration lesson. Kimberly walked the students through the process of the workshop, preparing them to plan and initiate their own pieces of writing. As she did, she saw to her horror that one of the observing teachers was sleeping, two were grading papers, and one was staring out the window. Two seemed to be paying attention, but one of them had a deep scowl on her face. It was a challenging audience. The lesson proceeded beautifully, however, and to Kimberly's amazement, the 90-minute literacy block ended with students talking excitedly in partners and then small groups about the short stories they would be working on for the next few class periods.

The group debriefing session immediately followed the demonstration. Kimberly had prepared a list of discussion questions for the teachers to think through what they had seen. "What did you notice about the lesson?" she asked the teachers timidly. "I noticed that the students can't spell at all," one teacher responded quickly. "Does this writer's workshop address that at all?" "I think the kids were so loud during the small-group discussion," another teacher stated. "What do we do to make them be quiet?" Kimberly held her breath and thought for a moment about how to proceed.

The session with third- and fourth-grade teachers was a shocking contrast. Kimberly did a demonstration lesson on literature circles. All six of the teachers sat attentively in the back taking notes. Several nodded their heads at different points in the lesson, scrawling furiously. Kimberly found these visual clues of the teachers' engagement encouraging, and her enthusiasm increased as the lesson proceeded. In the group debriefing session that followed, the teachers actually gave her a round of applause. The discussion that followed was intense as teachers asked questions, gave suggestions, and reflected upon how they would go about implementing this practice in their classrooms.

By the third round of demonstrations, Kimberly realized that the divide she had witnessed in the library between newer and experienced, lower- and upper-grade teachers was more than just a choice of where to sit in staff meetings. It was a deep cultural divide that was both a significant problem in the school climate and an impediment to coherence and school improvement.

A few days later, Kimberly and Principal Stillman sat with Liz Alvarez, a staff member from LLIC, discussing the cultural divide on the staff of Barley School. "I feel like we have hit a wall in our work," Kimberly told Liz. "What can we do to move forward?" The three continued to discuss possibilities. "Why don't we look at a list of all of your teachers and talk through the strengths and weaknesses of each," Liz suggested. "Perhaps we can identify some leaders in your teachers who can help you bring the school together." The three talked through the list. The fourth name on the list was Alana Taylor, a sixth-grade teacher. "Mrs. Taylor. Experienced. Resistant," Kimberly summarized. "Strengths?" Liz asked. "Runs a mentoring program that pairs sixth-grade students with third-grade students," Kimberly responded. "Maybe that is a point of connection," Principal Stillman said excitedly. "It is a program that links the upper and lower grades!" The three decided to try to build upon the mentor program, to expand the mentor program to include more grade levels. They worked together to pair all of the upper- and lower-grade classrooms.

At the next staff meeting, Kimberly, Principal Stillman, and Liz together described the mentoring program to the teachers. They asked Mrs. Taylor to stand up and talk about her vision for the program. Most teachers were attentive, and Kimberly immediately noticed that the group of experienced teachers seemed interested. As Mrs. Taylor described the program, Kimberly handed out the list of teachers who were to be paired together. Kimberly then described to the teachers the plan to integrate literacy work into the mentoring meetings. "The perfect way for our older students to really get a deeper understanding of reading and writing is for them to share and teach it," she explained to the teachers. To Kimberly's surprise, most teachers seemed to be nodding along with what she was saying. Kimberly handed out a list of literacy best practices that were modified for cross-age groupings, for example, literature circles for mixed-grade groups and writer's workshop sharing between mentoring pairs. "These are just my ideas," she said to the teachers. "You and your partnering teacher may have others that are even better."

The rest of the meeting was devoted to paired classroom teachers planning their mentoring program and the literacy work within it. Kimberly, Principal Stillman, and Liz circulated as the pairs talked, answering questions and providing encouragement.

Observations of the paired literacy mentoring activities over the coming months revealed some success. The children were so enthusiastic about the activities that the teachers at all levels began to get more excited. "I cannot believe my students love mentoring so much," an eighth-grade teacher told Kimberly. "They love their little brother or little sister and can't wait to work with them." The shared planning and conversation between the pairs helped to begin to bridge the gap between the more and less experienced teachers and the upper- and lower-grades and across racial lines. Most of the more experienced teachers got more excited. "I really think Mr. Trudy has some fantastic ideas," a fifth-grade teacher said about her second-grade colleague. In the end, all but two of the pairs of teachers worked productively together. "We made real progress this year," Liz stated to Kimberly as the two walked out of the school together on the last day of the school year. As the year came to a close, the best practices were taking root, the mentoring program was bridging the divide, and two teachers most resistant to the literacy program had decided to leave.

Challenge 2: Understanding Student Growth

Energized by the successes of her 1st year as literacy facilitator, Kimberly returned to school ready to move into the next round of her work. She aimed to deepen the literacy practices from the previous year. It was the 2nd week of school, and Kimberly sat at a table in the LLIC offices with four staff members from LLIC and Principal Stillman. "How are you feeling about last year?" asked Liz Alvarez. "I feel great," Kimberly responded. "We made a lot of progress, I think," Principal Stillman stated. As the meeting proceeded, it became clear that Liz was pushing toward something. "What is it, Liz?" asked Kimberly. Liz sighed and leveled with Kimberly and Principal Stillman. "We have to deepen the work at Barley School," Liz explained. "The literacy work is getting there, but teachers are not thinking deeply about assessing what students know and still need to learn."

The meeting continued, and the staff from LLIC walked through a list of strengths and weaknesses of the literacy work at Barley School. Kimberly left feeling deflated. "I thought we were doing so well until I saw this list. The list of weaknesses is twice as long as the strengths!" she said to Principal Stillman on the way back to Barley School. "Let's just focus on the assessments," Principal Stillman responded. "One thing, one day at a time."

Liz arrived at Barley School a few weeks later for the first of eight grade-level workshops on assessment. She sat at the table with the fourth-grade teachers. Kimberly ran the meeting. "We need to think about formative assessments, ways that we can judge what students know and still need to learn that can guide our work in literacy," she told the fourth-grade teachers. "Liz is here to help us to think about assessment."

Following the grade-level workshop, Kimberly, Liz, and Principal Stillman worked together to analyze the standardized test results in reading for Barley School's students. "Look at the achievement gains in grade seven, they are nonexistent," Kimberly stated, discouraged. "The students in third grade really have excellent reading comprehension," Principal Stillman stated. The trio continued to work, noting the uneven gains and progress in various grade levels. "What are we going to do to address these differences?" Kimberly asked Liz. "Now is the time to make these grade-level teams work for you," Liz responded.

Kimberly and Principal Stillman provided each grade-level team with an itemized analysis from the state reading test of the skills that students in the grade performed well on and the ones that they performed poorly on. The grade-level teams discussed ways to target the skills that needed work. In addition, the teams worked together to create a list of other tools they could use to formatively assess what their students knew and still needed to learn in literacy. Finally, they created a schedule for using the formative assessment tools to compare how their students were doing over the course of the year.

"The assessment work really is moving," Kimberly told Liz over the phone one day in late March. "Finally, the conversations are deepening." Before she had finished the sentence on the phone, Principal Stillman walked into Kimberly's office, frowning. "We need to talk," she said to Kimberly. "Now."

Kimberly quickly hung up the phone and followed Principal Stillman into her office. Two of the three sixth-grade teachers sat in chairs, waiting. "We are quitting," Mrs. Hill announced. "What?" Kimberly responded. "We are tired of being blamed for the low achievement," Mrs. Hill responded. "How can it be our fault and not the fault of the teachers in the grades below ours?" Mrs. Hill continued, describing a conversation that she overheard in the teachers' lounge. "The third-grade teachers all blamed us. They were like, we are doing fine, it is the sixth grade that is messing everything up," she paraphrased.

In response to the sixth-grade teachers' concerns, Principal Stillman brought in a professional facilitator to lead a schoolwide conversation. Principal Stillman framed the conversation as a time to "clear the air" and "be honest." Teachers took her seriously. Difficult issues were raised about perceptions of student abilities, race, class, and school history. The teachers reached an agreement about trying to not blame one another, but rather to think about assessment and student achievement jointly. Every grade level's success was everyone's success; every student failure was everyone's failure.

At the end of the year, one of the sixth-grade teachers ended up leaving anyway, despite Principal Stillman's attempt to resolve the issues in the schoolwide conversation. Kimberly felt that despite the challenges of the year, much progress had been made. "I am proud of our school," she stated. "We did some hard work this year."

Challenge 3: Deepening Peer Collaboration

Having laid the foundation for the use of best practices in literacy and assessment, Kimberly began her 3rd year as the facilitator with excitement. The goal in her 3rd year, she and Liz discussed, was to move more of the impetus for the literacy work into the roles and lives of teachers. "This is their work, they have to own it," Liz stated.

Kimberly stood before the staff at the second staff meeting of the year. "I am here to talk about our literacy work," Kimberly stated. "What do we want to do this year?" The staff chatted excitedly about the new best practices in literacy that LLIC had suggested for the continuing work. "I would really like to see demonstration lessons included again," Mrs. Halsey stated. Murmurs of agreement echoed throughout the library. "That sounds great," Kimberly responded. "Who would like to give them?" The teachers sat in stunned silence. "Isn't that your job?" Mrs. Smith asked. "Now is the time to deepen this work, expand the leadership to more teachers," Principal Stillman responded.

Kimberly found herself knocking on doors, begging for volunteers. "Please, Mrs. Halsey, you are among the best teachers in the building," Kimberly coaxed. "You can do this, I can help you prepare the demo lesson." Mrs. Halsey sighed and reluctantly agreed.

Several weeks later, the fourth- and fifth-grade teachers were meeting after Mrs. Halsey's demonstration lesson. The teachers sat in silence, uncertain who was to begin. "Well, doesn't anyone have anything to say about it?" Mrs. Halsey finally asked. The room was quiet, and several teachers looked at the floor. "I thought it was good," one teacher finally responded. More silence. "We have to dig a little deeper," Kimberly gently pushed. "What were the strengths? What were the weaknesses? What did you like about this approach? What did you not like?" The group continued to struggle to communicate as Kimberly tried to step back and allow them to collaborate without her lead. "I don't mean you did it wrong," one teacher told Mrs. Halsey. "It just wasn't the way I would have done it." Kimberly held her breath as she waited for Mrs. Halsey to respond. "I am never doing this again!" Mrs. Halsey sighed. "I feel like a bad teacher."

Similar situations erupted at other grade levels. Peers struggled to learn how to work together without offending one another. Several of the sessions erupted into arguments. Kimberly called Liz for help. "How do I manage this?" Kimberly asked Liz. "You have to let them grow into it," Liz explained. "They are used to you being the one to take the risks in the demo lessons and you leading the reflection. They will get it if you step back."

Several months later, Kimberly realized Liz had been right. The groups had learned to work together in a more productive manner. Though the conversations were painful, the teachers were getting there.

Conclusion

As the 4th year of the literacy intervention drew to a close, Kimberly felt proud of the work she had done at Barley School. Reading achievement was on the rise at the school; the trend was clear both in the formative assessments and on the state test. Teacher conversations were fundamentally different than they had been just a few years before. In all, about a third of the teachers had turned over since Principal Stillman arrived. The most resistant teachers had left almost entirely.

But while the accomplishments were many, Kimberly knew that challenges still remained in continuing to deepen the literacy work at Barley School. Several grade levels were not making the desired level of progress in student achievement. The literacy work did not seem to be translating into gains across the board in other subjects the way that Principal Stillman had hoped. There was more work to be done at Barley School.

And as the school year closed, the next chapter in the story of Barley School would take place without Kimberly there to lead the literacy initiative. Kimberly had been recruited to take a central office coaching position and had decided to accept it. "The work is never really done," Kimberly reflected with Liz in the pair's final meeting at Barley School. "No," Liz responded. "It certainly isn't."

Barley Teaching Notes

ACTIVITY. CASE ANALYSIS

Objective: To analyze the case of Barley School using literature on change theory and scaling up reform. Our analysis will include four steps:

1. Establishing the facts of the case.
2. Analyze the case using literature on the change process.
3. Analyze the case using literature on scaling up reform.

4. Writing a letter to the literacy facilitator at Barley School as a culminating activity.

Each of these steps is elaborated below.

Step 1. Establishing the Facts of the Case

Begin by recalling the facts of the case using Table 3.1 in the Appendix as a guide. This process will help you establish what is known and unknown about the case. Be careful to distinguish between known facts and presumptions.

Further solidify your understanding of the case by comparing your list of facts with those of another classmate. Clarify and reconcile any areas of disagreement or inconsistency. When you feel confident that you know the facts of the case, proceed to Step 2.

Step 2. Analysis: The Change Process

The second step in analyzing the case of Barley School is to consider the change process underlying the reforms that are taking place. Read the article by Michael Fullan and Matthew Miles (1992) and complete the activities below.

READING 1

Fullan, M. G., & Miles, M. B. (1992). Getting reform right: What works and what doesn't. *Phi Delta Kappan, 73*(10), 744–752.

In this article Fullan and Miles outline a list of reasons why reforms fail and present a set of propositions for successful reform. The authors' claims provide a frame for examining the change process at Barley School. To systematically analyze the case from the perspective of change theory, complete the following activities.

Part 1. First, consider "Why Reforms Fail":

1. On your own, take brief notes on *Why Reforms Fail*. To facilitate your understanding, try to capture the main ideas in your own words.
2. Then, using the grid in Table 3.2 in the Appendix as a guide, apply the concepts presented by Fullan and Miles to the case of Barley School. Which aspects of the reform strategy at Barley fall into the categories of reform failure defined by the authors?
3. In small groups, discuss the completed tables.

Part 2. Second, consider the authors' "Propositions for Success":

4. On your own, take brief notes on *Propositions for Success*. To facilitate your understanding, try to capture the main ideas in your own words.
5. Then, using the grid in Table 3.3 in the Appendix as a guide, apply the concepts presented by Fullan and Miles to the case of Barley School. Which aspects of the reform strategy at Barley fall into the propositions for success defined by the authors?
6. In small groups, discuss the completed tables.

Step 3. Analysis: Scaling Up to Promote Deep Change

The third step in analyzing the case of Barley School is to consider the process of "scaling up" reform and its connection to promoting deep change. Read the article by Coburn (2003) and complete the activities below.

READING 2

Coburn, C. E. (2003). Rethinking scale: Moving beyond numbers to deep and lasting change. *Educational Researcher, 32*(6), 3–12.

In *Rethinking Scale*, Coburn argues that the concept of scale is imperfect because of the "unidimensional" definition as the "numbers of schools reached by a given reform effort." Coburn argues for an expanded definition of scale with a focus on classroom instruction, sustainability, norms, beliefs, and shifts in ownership.

   Part 1. In small groups, discuss each of the four key concepts defined by Coburn: *depth, sustainability, spread of norms,* and *shift in reform ownership.* How do you understand each of the concepts? Discuss any differences of interpretation that exist in your group.

   Part 2. Apply each of the four key concepts to the case of Barley School. How is each manifested in the case? Could changes in the depth, sustainability, spread of norms, and shift in reform ownership at Barley deepen Kimberly's work? Discuss your opinions and interpretations.

Step 4. Culminating Activity: A Letter to the Literacy Facilitator at Barley School

The final step is to write a letter to the new literacy facilitator who will take over Kimberly's work at Barley School. Write from Kimberly's perspective.

The purpose of the letter is to share your insights from 4 years of working at Barley. You hope to ease your replacement's transition and help him or her avoid mistakes you may have made. Most importantly, your letter should explicitly identify a set of strategies that your replacement might use to deepen the change process and increase the scale of the literacy facilitator's work. Explain the rationale behind your suggestions.

Sexton School District

PART ONE: THE DISTRICT CONTEXT

This fictionalized case study based on a real school district situates the work of the math coach within the context of the district's history, culture, demographics, and reform policies. In this section of the case you will learn about the district-level reform efforts as a backdrop to school-level reform.

The Community

Sexton School District is located in a densely populated area of the mid-Atlantic United States. Sexton, a town with 50,000 residents, is marked by stark contrasts. The east side of town contains multimillion-dollar Victorian homes whose owners commute daily to a major metropolitan city to work at high-paying jobs in business and finance. On the west side of town, more modest Victorian homes have been divided into multifamily residences with fire escapes draped across peeling facades. To punctuate the differences between east and west, a defunct railroad trestle bisects the two sections of town. The most recent census describes Sexton's population as 60% African American, 30% Latino, and 10% White. In the words of the mayor, "We are a community of great racial, cultural, and economic diversity."

In recent years, this diversity has been the source of tension in Sexton. The local paper has run a series of articles documenting conflict between the Latino and African American communities. At the heart of this conflict is the high unemployment rate in Sexton, which registers at twice the national average. Competition for scarce jobs has exacerbated perceived differences between longtime residents and more recent newcomers. Accusations of disrespect have eroded trust on both sides.

The local paper has also been publishing results from the new standardized student assessments. Provocative headlines such as "SCHOOLS FAILING" and "SCORES DOWN AGAIN" have created a stir in the community. Letters to the editor ask, "What happened to our schools?" and community organizers have urged citizens to attend the monthly school board meetings to express their concerns. In the context of reduced employment prospects, low student performance on highly visible exams magnifies existing tensions felt in the community.

110

The School District

The Central Office is located near Main Street in a three-story building that would have been a handsome single-family home earlier in the century. The wide front porch is decorated with a simple sign that identifies the building as part of the public schools. Nearly all of the district administrators who work in the central office have been longtime educators in the Sexton Public School District. Few have worked in any other district. Historically, the central office administrators have performed fairly predictable work: hiring new teachers, managing school budgets, and monitoring facilities operations.

The Sexton Public School District enrolls 70% of Sexton's school-aged children. The remaining 30% attend parochial or private school. Of the approximately 8,500 public school students, 71% are African American and 28% are Latino. 70% of the public school population qualifies for free or reduced-price lunch. 17% of the student population has limited English proficiency.

The district includes 10 K–5 elementary schools ranging from 250 to 450 students each. The two middle schools serve students in grades 6–8 and service 700 and 950 students respectively. The single high school has a population of nearly 2,000. While the 1960s-era high school is spacious and fairly modern, the elementary schools are cramped and lacking modern facilities.

The nearly 600 teachers who work in Sexton are a mixed group. Approximately half the teachers live in Sexton and have deep roots in the community. For many of these teachers, education seems to run in the family. It is common to find the same family name listed repeatedly on the employee directory, and newcomers are often surprised to learn that siblings teach in the same building or that the role of principal has passed from one generation to the next. These kinship relationships create a sense of familiarity and continuity in the schools. The other half of Sexton's teachers commute from nearby towns. This group is a mixture of novice and veteran teachers, and their rate of turnover tends to be higher than the resident teachers'.

In recent years, all of the schools in Sexton have reported increases in the number of altercations between students. Some of the conflicts at the high school have been described as "gang-related," and some students have been found carrying box cutters to school. Even in the elementary schools, classroom disruptions seem to be on the rise, prompting teachers to raise concerns about student behavior. One teacher expressed the sentiments of many: "How am I supposed to teach these kids when they're bouncing off the walls?" Not surprisingly, parents have also become more vocal, raising concerns about school safety, poor classroom management, and student underperformance. "What are they doing with those kids all day to get such low test scores? Our kids aren't dumb!"

New Leadership

This was the atmosphere that greeted newly appointed superintendent Frank Fulton when he arrived in August for what would become an 8-year tenure as the district's reform-minded leader. Dr. Fulton had spent the previous 3 years working for the state department of education as the Assistant Commissioner and Director of Urban Education. Prior to that he had served as superintendent of a nearby district for 5 years, and his earlier work in education had been as a principal and classroom teacher. These experiences, along with a string of degrees from prestigious universities, had made him a popular candidate for the position. The fact that he was African American and a native of the state further endeared him to Sexton residents and the school board.

In the 1st year of his superintendency Dr. Fulton spent time talking to school staff, principals, parents, and community members. These conversations led him to believe that Sexton School District had a "toxic culture" characterized by a fractured spirit and negativity. Plagued by inertia, apathy, cynicism, misinformation, and defensiveness, the school system was unable to respond to student or community needs.

At the same time, Dr. Fulton also learned that the Sexton community was deeply committed to its schools. They wanted a role in shaping the district and they demanded a stronger partnership between the community and the schools. To forge stronger connections, Dr. Fulton established a series of Community Engagement Forums. These monthly forums took place throughout Dr. Fulton's 2nd year on the job, running from September through June. The educational forums were intended to provide the community with information about the design and organization of high-quality schools. Dr. Fulton invited highly regarded speakers to participate in panels dedicated to topics such as urban education, community–school partnerships, standards-based instruction, and academic excellence. The forums provided the community with much-needed information. They also directed the conversation toward a more positive, empowered approach to thinking about school reform. Dr. Fulton wanted to minimize the tendency to get trapped in a cycle of blame and accusation. Rather than pointing fingers, he wanted the community to imagine what could be and to take collective responsibility for realizing their potential.

Reforming the System

Although Dr. Fulton was committed to involving the community in reforming the education system, he also had a vision of the kind of education system he wanted to cultivate. At the heart of his vision was a belief that all children should have access to a high-quality educational experience. "This is a matter of social justice," he explained at a board meeting. "All children deserve the opportunity to succeed. Everything we do should be driven by what's best for kids." With this in mind, Dr. Fulton articulated a *12-Step Framework for Reform* that was widely circulated within the community:

1. Rethinking of district vision, mission, and beliefs to ensure the success of every child.
2. Development of student learning and performance standards that clearly indicate what students should know and be able to do.
3. Development of assessment and accountability systems to measure student progress and school/district effectiveness.
4. Implementation of policies, procedures, and practices to decentralize decision-making to the school site to the maximum extent possible.
5. Redefinition of roles, responsibilities, and functions to support and empower staff to make the major decisions affecting the teaching and learning process in the school.
6. Utilization of research-driven, data-based approaches to give direction to initiatives to improve teaching and learning processes.
7. Expansion of the role of technology in all school district operations (instructional, administrative and management, student data management).
8. Establishment of a partnership between union and management to promote and expect shared responsibility for the education of children and the establishment of relationships based upon mutual respect, trust, and accountability.
9. Partnerships with parents, community, social and health service agencies, businesses, churches, and government at all levels (municipal, county, state, and federal) to ensure comprehensive support for students and their learning needs.
10. Improvement of communication strategies and systems to engage all internal and external stakeholder groups in the ongoing work and mission of the public schools of Sexton.
11. Organization and maintenance of systemic efforts to engage parents in the education of their children and the work of the schools and district.
12. Establishment of a comprehensive staff development system aimed at the professionalization of teaching and learning in the public schools of Sexton.

Dr. Fulton spoke passionately to the school board about the importance of moving forward purposefully and steadily to address all 12 steps. He acknowledged the challenges but also admonished, "Nothing worth doing is easy." To mark the inception of Sexton's reform efforts, Dr. Fulton convened a voluntary group of educators and community members to work collaboratively to develop a mission statement that would guide their short- and long-term improvement efforts. Together they agreed:

> The Sexton Public Schools, in partnership with its community, shall do whatever it takes for every student to achieve high academic standards. No alibis! No excuses! No exceptions!

After 2 years on the job, Dr. Fulton was ready to move forward with his reform agenda.

A Strategic Plan

At the start of Dr. Fulton's 3rd year on the job the community was ready to embrace change. Mandatory standardized student performance assessments made it easy to see that Sexton's students were lagging behind. In the words of the local paper, students' scores were "abysmal." On average, 28% of fourth-grade students received scores of proficient or higher in mathematics. Only 17% of eighth-graders scored proficient or higher on the math assessment. Scores for literacy were only slightly better. In comparison with other students in the state, Sexton's students were among the lowest-performing. Everyone in the community agreed that significant changes would need to take place in order to improve student achievement.

At the same time, a state-sponsored audit revealed that Sexton School District had some of the lowest per-pupil funding in the state. The use of property taxes to fund schools and the school funding formula made it difficult for the district to adequately finance public education. The effects were clear: buildings were in disrepair, teachers lacked qualifications, and improvement efforts were discordant and piecemeal. As such, Sexton became eligible for supplemental state funds. This new state program was intended to provide low-income districts with the resources needed to engage in systemic reform and build capacity in their schools. The funds would be available as long as the district qualified and the funds were used for state-approved improvement efforts, including: 1) adoption of a comprehensive reform model, 2) standards-based instruction, 3) professional development for teachers, 4) formative and summative assessments, 5) facilities improvements, and 6) technological upgrades.

Dr. Fulton charged the principals with developing a strategic plan for reform that would conform to the state requirements and the district's mission. The principals from all 13 schools conducted needs assessments in their schools, sought feedback from teachers, and worked collaboratively to identify a set of reforms that the schools could implement. These strategic planning conversations often lasted late into the night as the administrators hashed out their beliefs about school improvement and the change process. All of the strategic planning meetings were facilitated by a pair of education scholars from the local university. The two professors worked skillfully to diffuse tensions and redirect the administrators' focus when they fell into old patterns of blame and accusation. By keeping the conversations focused on shared goals, the principals devised a 5-year strategic plan that incorporated all six of the state's reform components.

While the principals hammered out a strategic plan, Dr. Fulton continued to exhort the values of collaboration and community. He spoke to all the school faculties, wrote letters to the editor, addressed the city council, and spoke to local civic organizations. Despite the changing venue, his message was always the same:

> The African American and Latino communities have a long tradition as community organizers. We take pride in our families, our churches, our communities. *Together* we must uphold our values. *Together* we must confront injustices. And *together* we must improve our schools. For too long we have failed these children. No one, and I mean no one, loves these children more than we do. It will not be easy but *together* we can improve their future. Together! No alibis! No excuses! No exceptions!

Dr. Fulton's heartfelt message appealed to the community's sense of pride, while simultaneously delivering the hard truth of misdirected energy and failure. Over and over again, his tough love message was met with applause and enthusiasm. "Together! No alibis! No excuses! No exceptions!" became the mantra heard all over Sexton.

PART TWO: SCHOOL-LEVEL REFORM

In this section of the case you will learn about some of the steps taken in Sexton to reform their system of education. In particular, you will learn about the comprehensive school reform model that the district adopted and how it paved the way for the math coach role.

Comprehensive Reform

A key component of Sexton School District's 5-year strategic plan was the adoption of a comprehensive school reform model. The administration reasoned that their schools would benefit from external assistance aimed at districtwide program coherence and systemic change. During their planning, the principals brought in representatives from three different companies who presented their models for comprehensive reform. Faculties at each elementary and middle school voted for their preferred model. Dr. Fulton encouraged the principals and teachers to select the model that would best support the districtwide literacy program they had recently adopted.

When the votes were tabulated, six of the elementary schools and one middle school reached an 80% majority vote to implement America's Choice School Design. Together, these seven schools became the first district-level cohort. The following year, an additional two elementary schools and the second middle school would also vote to adopt the America's Choice model, becoming the second district-level cohort. The remaining two elementary schools and the high school would not reach the majority vote necessary for model adoption, although they would eventually incorporate many of the practices associated with America's Choice schools as a result of exposure to the reforms in district-level professional development workshops. The America's Choice School Design focused on "five critical elements of school improvement" (see http://www.americaschoice.org/schooldesign):

1. Creating a standards-based system with assessments that monitor progress and inform instruction.
2. Aligning instruction to standards and focusing teaching on moving students from where they are to where they need to be.
3. Strengthening instructional leadership.
4. Building professional learning communities.
5. Engaging parents and the community.

Each of these design elements aimed at building school capacity for improvement.

The implementation of the America's Choice School Design model began immediately. Over the summer teachers were paid to attend professional development related to understanding the model, learning how to align instruction to the state standards, and using standards-based assessments. Principals also received training in how to build broad-based leadership, structure schedules for maximum collaboration, and create school environments in which parents would feel welcome. Principals in each school, with the assistance of the district administrators, selected a full-time design coach from within their staff who would be responsible for communicating with the America's Choice representative and coordinating implementation of the model. In addition, literacy coaches were selected for each school. The literacy coaches were responsible for implementing the district's literacy program as well as literacy-based components of America's Choice School Design, including reader's and writer's workshops, author studies, and book-of-the-month activities. After 2 years of implementation, the literacy scores in the America's Choice schools had doubled and the district began looking for ways to expand their success.

Math Reform

While the literacy scores increased, the math scores stayed the same. In response to this stagnation, a district-level committee was created to review math curricula and select a new program that would support standards-based math instruction. The options were quickly whittled down to three choices. A number of the committee members expressed strong support for Math Investigations, a constructivist inquiry-based approach to math instruction. In particular, the district-level math supervisor, Marge Hansen, and math education representatives from two different universities were strong advocates of Investigations, referring to it as the most rigorous and intensive of the three programs. The committee members acknowledged that the level of math content knowledge necessary to implement Investigations would be high. As a result, the district made a commitment to fund math coach roles that would be modeled after the literacy coaches.

As anticipated, the new math program presented a steep learning curve for everyone in the district. The previous math program had offered a traditional approach to learning, focusing on math algorithms that the students would memorize and apply. Under the new program, procedural rules were replaced with an inquiry-based approach that aimed at comprehension of mathematical concepts. Instead of focusing on getting the "right answer," students were to develop multiple techniques for solving problems, explain their logic, and represent their ideas pictorially. Teachers had to shift from marking "right" or "wrong" to examining students' problem-solving processes and identifying the misconceptions in students' thinking. More time was spent on understanding *why* the wrong answers were wrong.

Math Reform at Carver Elementary

Carver Elementary School is emblematic of Dr. Fulton's vision for all of the schools in Sexton School District. Long a fixture on the west side, Carver's new facility was built with some of the supplemental funds awarded by the state. In keeping with Dr. Fulton's vision, Carver's new building was designed as a community school. The two-story building is bright and spacious, with wide hallways and classrooms clustered in grade-level pods. The library is colorful and modern, with multicultural artwork, a mini-amphitheater for group storytelling, and a separate computer lab. A staircase at the center of the school opens onto a large indoor courtyard. Skylights illuminate a floor-to-ceiling mural that occupies three walls. The professionally painted mural depicts Sexton's neighborhoods, cultures, holiday festivals, historic buildings, ordinary citizens, and local celebrities.

Just as impressive as the building are Carver's community-oriented programs. A small health clinic provides basic services to both children and adults. Classes for English language learners are offered weekly to adult learners who can take advantage of free child care. A popular learn-to-read program for adults is staffed by community volunteers and services nearly 50 community members. Before- and afterschool educational programs are available to Carver's 350 students, and numerous community organizations use the facilities for their meetings and social gatherings.

When Math Investigations was adopted, the teachers at Carver had been working with the America's Choice School Design for 2 years. Structures had been created to promote greater teacher collaboration around instruction, including weekly grade-level meetings and afterschool in-service dedicated to instructional improvement. Although the teachers were leery about taking on another new program, they recognized that the math scores were unsatisfactory. "Our test scores indicate that something is missing, we just aren't sure what it is." Thus, the teachers signed up to attend 1 or 2 weeks of training in Math Investigations prior to the start of the school year and to fully implement Investigations in all grade levels starting in September.

The math coach for Carver Elementary was Connie Sayles. Connie had expressed her interest in the position as soon it was posted. Over the 22 years she had worked at Carver, Connie had often been the go-to person for math. Although Connie's master's degree was actually in reading, she enjoyed math and didn't mind helping her colleagues who were less mathematically inclined. The other teachers described her as mild-mannered and unflappable. "She's been here forever," one of the younger teachers remarked, "nothing fazes her." For her part, Connie knew that the teachers were unsure about math reform, but she felt certain her long-standing status and good rapport would carry her through the inevitable bumps and challenges. "Everyone knows we need to do something. As long as I can help the teachers through it, I'm sure we'll come out on the other end," she remarked.

When Connie received the official letter confirming her new role, she also learned that she would work under the supervision of the new assistant principal, Mr. Brown. Mr. Brown had been hired from a neighboring district where he had worked as the principal of a middle school. His reasons for working in Sexton were twofold. "I live here in Sexton and my daughter goes to school in the district. I knew Dr. Fulton was shaking up the system and I wanted to be a part of that." Prior to becoming a principal, Mr. Brown had been a teacher for 10 years. Although he thought of himself as more literacy-oriented, he had been told during the interview that he would be expected to oversee the math program implementation. Mr. Brown took it upon himself to learn about elementary math in general and Math Investigations in particular. In addition to taking an online math course, he enrolled in professional development offered by the state Association for Teachers of Math and, along with Connie, attended both weeks of the Math Investigations teacher training over the summer.

Together Mr. Brown and Connie collaborated to work out a common understanding of the math coach role. "Essentially, my job is to provide support for the teachers so that they can implement Investigations as it was intended," Connie explained to teachers. According to Mr. Brown, "She runs grade-level meetings every other week, models lessons, helps teachers use task specific rubrics and take anecdotal notes, reviews the commentary that teachers make on students' work, and checks to make sure that appropriate student work is on display." Both Connie and Mr. Brown were pleased with the working relationship they had developed and felt hopeful that the momentum that had made literacy reform so successful would carry over to math.

Implementation

Right from the start, the teachers at Carver demanded Connie's assistance. They left notes in her mailbox, sent e-mail messages, stopped her in the hallway, and lined up outside her office first thing in the morning. "Will you show me how to do a 10-minute mini-lesson?" "Should I do anecdotal notes with all the kids?" "Where do I get more base ten blocks?" "How will they learn their math facts if we're using calculators?" In every case, Connie responded patiently, giving advice, providing necessary materials, or offering to model in the teacher's classroom. Before long, Connie had a full schedule of model lessons.

Although Connie was spending time in classrooms, she wasn't sure the teachers were deepening their math practice. Over the course of the year, Connie had noticed that the teachers continued to ask about logistics or technical issues. They seldom asked questions related to math content, and many of their queries conveyed ongoing confusion about the shift to an inquiry-based teaching approach.

> When teachers ask me why we're allowing the kids to count on their fingers or why we no longer teach them to "carry the one" in two-digit addition, I realize that they really don't understand the purpose of the math program. Their mind-set is still rooted in procedural

math. They can't quite make sense of the concept-oriented instructional strategies.

Connie's belief that the teachers "don't really get it" was further confirmed in the grade-level meetings. For each of the sessions Connie was careful to outline an agenda with specific goals and norms for interaction. At the top of each agenda she prominently typed the district's mission statement—"no alibis, no exceptions, no excuses." She structured each meeting around the evaluation of student work. "By looking at student assessments," she reasoned, "we can use data to drive instructional change." Yet it had been difficult to keep the conversation focused on learning and teaching. With each passing week teachers became more inclined to dismiss the sample work in favor of sharing their experiences teaching Math Investigations.

At her most recent first-grade meeting, the conversation had turned into a story-swapping session more quickly than usual. One teacher shared, "My ten-minute mini-lesson turned into an hour-long endeavor! To add thirty plus ten Carlos drew forty supersonic jets. At this rate we'll never cover all the content standards." Another teacher chimed in, "When I asked them to explain their answers I got a sea of blank stares. First-graders aren't able to articulate that kind of reasoning. It's just not realistic." This prompted another teacher to add, "These kids will be in fourth grade and asking for teddy bear counters. Learning is supposed to be hard work. Life isn't all fun and games." Instead of talking about math content, student learning, and instructional strategies, the teachers had begun to use the grade-level meetings as an opportunity to confirm negative assumptions. And their like-minded colleagues were quick to offer support.

Connie herself was conflicted. On one hand, the teachers seemed to have some legitimate concerns. Implementing the Investigations program was much more time-consuming than their previous "workbook approach" to teaching math. And the lessons did seem more demanding of students. It was true that most of their students had never taken a long trip or ridden a bicycle. Could their kids do this kind of problem-solving the way kids in more affluent districts could? And recently, Connie had begun to hear complaints from parents about the homework activities. "What's this about rolling dice?" asked one mother. "I don't send my son to school to play dice. He's there to learn math facts!"

PART THREE: BUILDING SUPPORTS FOR REFORM

In this section of the case you will learn about the ways in which Sexton School District worked to build supports for the math coaches. Despite these supports, the coaches continued to be challenged in their new roles.

District-Level Support

Following the 1st year of implementation it was clear that the math program would need additional supports beyond the work of the math coaches. Reports from principals and math coaches suggested that implementation was spotty and that teachers seemed less open-minded about the program than they had been the previous summer. Marge Hansen, the district-level math supervisor, agreed with the coaches' assessment that teachers didn't understand the reasoning behind the concept-oriented, inquiry-based program. She also believed that part of the problem was the coaches' own level of content knowledge.

> We need to scale up implementation in each of the buildings. And the coaches are at differing levels as far as their own mathematical understanding. So part of our work is scaling up the coaches' mathematics even though they're not all aware they need it.

In preparation for the 2nd year of Math Investigations implementation, Marge talked with the principals about the possibility of pulling coaches out of their schools one afternoon each week for professional development at the central office. The principals agreed that the time spent out of the building would be worthwhile if coach effectiveness increased. Marge planned to facilitate the 3-hour sessions with the help of an external math consultant and one of the math educators from a local university. The purpose of the sessions would be to learn about math and talk about issues related to pedagogy. "The coaches' knowledge of pedagogy has a direct transfer to the pedagogy of the classroom teachers."

In addition, Marge planned to have monthly afterschool meetings with the principals. "For this to work there needs to be constant articulation between administrators, myself, my director, principals, and math coaches. We need to be on the same page in terms of what this role looks like and the work that the coaches should be doing in schools." Marge knew of several instances when math coaches had been asked to substitute for absent teachers, order materials, or perform administrative duties. Although she didn't think it was happening frequently, it was a practice she wanted to curtail. "The math coaches' role is to support the teachers' ability to implement the math program at high levels in their classrooms. Not to help principals manage the school."

Professional Development for Math Coaches

At the first professional development session of the year Marge explained her intentions for the work they would be doing together. "We know that

the first year of any program you're really focusing on the management and the details and the how-do-you-do-its. Now that we're going into the second year, we really need to be shifting the focus into studying the mathematics." Then Marge introduced Carol, the external consultant from Math Investigations.

Carol began by arranging the twelve participants—the ten coaches, Marge, and the math educator—into three groups: one group of three, a group of four, and one group of five. Then she asked the group members to find one thing they had in common with each other group member. The coaches quickly identified facts about themselves such as the month of their birth and favorite hobbies. Then Carol asked, "If each group member has one thing in common with every other group member, how many commonalities are there across your group?" Carol paused. "Another way to think about it is, if each of you shook hands with every member of your group just one time, how many times would you shake hands?"

Each group got busy. The group of five began acting out the problem. After the first person shook hands with everyone that person was effectively "out." With each successive round of handshaking another person was "out." On a piece of chart paper somebody wrote: 4+3+2+1=10. One coach explained, "Each round of handshaking results in a number that is one less than the previous round." Then Carol asked each of the groups to share their answers. Some groups demonstrated how they had solved the problem. Next Carol asked, "What would the answer be for a group of twenty-five?" Again, the groups began to work through the process, looking for a formula that would allow them to arrive at the answer.

One group wrote: $24 + 23 + 22 + 21 + 20 \ldots 5 + 4 + 3 + 2 + 1$. The group members agreed that the first and last numbers add up to 25. The second and second-to-last numbers also add up to 25, and so on. "There are twelve sets like this (half of twenty-four). So multiplying twelve times twenty-five results in the answer: three hundred." Then the groups took turns sharing their answers and explaining the method they had used. Each group had applied a different process to arrive at the same answer. Coaches around the room shook their heads in amazement. Although all groups arrived at the correct answer, some got closer to discerning a mathematical formula. Carol offered one more example from a group she had worked with previously in which the members had arrived at the wrong answer.

At the conclusion of the hourlong exercise, Carol asked the coaches to reflect on the process that they had gone through and how she had coordinated it. She asked the coaches to consider why she had shown them the wrong answer after they had already determined a formula. One coach volunteered that it prompted them to think about their answers in a different way and to test their knowledge. Carol confided that she hadn't been sure the group would want to discuss the wrong answer. "That would have been okay, too. It would have been an indicator of where you are at in your math learning." Carol pointed out the value in *not* starting with the best or most complete answer. "Why are we as teachers so quick to call on the student with the right answer?" she asked. One coach replied that there was too much content to cover and pressure to prepare for the test. Heads around the room nodded in agreement. Another coach asked if Carol had considered the order in which she asked the groups to present. "Definitely," she replied. "But remember, the art of delivery takes a long time to develop, so we need to be careful not to be too harsh with teachers who haven't yet mastered the ability to determine who should go first." In conclusion, Carol stated, "Consider whether you could adapt this activity for use with the teachers in your school."

Implementation Continued

At the conclusion of the 2nd year of implementation, everyone agreed that the coaches had made progress in their understanding of mathematics. Reflecting on her experience, one coach explained, "This role is so new. I don't always know what I'm doing. Being able to talk with other coaches from other buildings has been a godsend. I feel much more confident now than I did in the beginning." Connie Sayles was equally pleased with her experience. "It's been a lot of fun getting to do math. I have a better sense now of how much more there is to know and a better understanding of how overwhelmed teachers can feel with the new program."

Marge agreed. "We've made a lot of progress. When I walk into classrooms I see a higher level of student engagement and student discourse. The mathematical thinking that is coming out of these children is wonderful." Another source of encouragement has been the state standardized test scores, which indicated modest increases in students' math performance, particularly in the area of problem-solving. "We are starting to see changes, but until we really bump up the scores on the state tests people are going to continue to scream and complain. We know it's going to take every bit of five years for that to happen, but that's not what folks want to hear." The slow rate of change continued to be a source of frustration for teachers, parents, and the community.

In fact, a small group of vocal parents had been complaining that the new math program neglected basic skills. A petition had been circulated requesting that the board review the adequacy of the program. Some of the impetus for the complaints had actually come from teachers. "There are a few teachers going out into the community and planting negative ideas," explained Marge. "It has been very, very frustrating. Dr. Fulton has made it clear to principals and teachers that such behavior is intolerable and will not be accepted, but we're still experiencing a small backlash." In response to the community concerns, Marge had begun to work with the coaches to plan a series of Family Math events for parents and caregivers. She hoped that increased communication with the community would yield greater support for the changes they were trying to make.

In general, Marge remained confident that the math program was the best fit for the district. Her main concerns continued to revolve around the coaches' level of math understanding. While the coaches were enthusiastic about the weekly professional development sessions, they didn't always stay focused on pedagogical issues the way Marge would have liked them to.

> The coaches continue to get involved in issues that are more administrative, like details about the standards-based report card. It's very important that they understand how the report card relates to the math program, but they have a tendency to get involved in the logistical issues. My response has been, "That's not your problem." I'd like them to be looking at scaling up their mathematics so they can help scale up teachers' mathematics.

Ironically, the challenge that Marge faced in trying to keep the focus on pedagogy was the same challenge the coaches faced in their grade-level meetings.

Thinking forward to the 3rd year of implementation, Marge had decided to add an additional component to the weekly professional development sessions. In addition to learning math content, the coaches would also learn how to effectively deliver that content to teachers. "All the coaches have grown in their understanding, but in the implementation of the math units there is still a lot of math that's sliding. The challenge comes from the coaches not being able to dig in deeply enough with the teachers." Marge recognized that it had been difficult for the coaches to have open conversations with the teachers about areas for improvement. Yet they would have to get to that step in order to fundamentally change pedagogical norms. Marge had begun to investigate different protocols the coaches might use to structure and guide difficult conversations. Critical Friends Groups and Collaborative Analysis of Student Learning seemed like two promising approaches that Marge planned to examine further.

"This time next year," Marge thought to herself, "we'll really start to see the results of our work."

Sexton Teaching Notes

ACTIVITY. CASE ANALYSIS

Objective: To analyze the case of Sexton School District using literature on the importance of capacity building and coherence in school reform. Our analysis will include four steps:

1. Establish the facts of the case.
2. Analyze the case using literature on capacity building.
3. Analyze using literature on instructional program coherence.
4. Write the final section of the Sexton case study as a culminating activity.

Each of these steps is elaborated below.

Step 1. Establishing the Facts of the Case

Begin by recalling the facts of the case using the Table 3.4 in the Appendix as a guide. This process will help you establish what is known and unknown about the case. Be careful to distinguish between known facts and presumptions.

Further solidify your understanding of the case by comparing your list of facts with those of another classmate. Clarify and reconcile any areas of disagreement or inconsistency. When you feel confident that you know the facts of the case proceed to Step 2.

Step 2. Analysis: Capacity Building

The second step in analyzing the case of Sexton School District is to reflect on the district's efforts to build school capacity to make and sustain change. To help you examine and assess Sexton's efforts read the policy brief by Massell (2000) and complete the activities below.

READING 1

Massell, D. (2000). *The district role in building capacity: Four strategies* (CPRE Research Brief NO. RB-32). Philadelphia: Consortium for Policy Research in Education.

In this policy brief, Massell uses research to identify and describe four strategies used by 22 districts in 8 states to build school capacity: 1) interpreting and using data, 2) building teacher knowledge and skills, 3) aligning curriculum and instruction, and 4) targeting interventions on low-performing students and/or schools.

Part 1. Review the case for evidence of the four capacity building strategies outlined by Massell (2000).

Part 2. With a partner or in small groups discuss ways in which Sexton School District could improve its capacity building efforts. Are some strategies under-developed? What steps need to be taken to further build capacity to make and sustain change?

Step 3. Analysis: Instructional Program Coherence

The second step in analyzing the case of Sexton School District is to consider the nature of the reforms taking place and the extent to which they reflect instructional program coherence as described in the article by Newmann, Smith, Allensworth, and Bryk (2001).

READING 1

Newmann, F. M., Smith, B., Allensworth, E., & Bryk, A. S. (2001). Instructional program coherence: What it is & why it should guide school improvement policy. *Educational Evaluation and Policy Analysis, 23*(4), 297–321.

In this research article, Newmann and his colleagues report that educational reforms that include high levels of instructional program coherence are more likely to result in improvements in student achievement. In addition, the authors report on a set of factors that facilitate instructional program coherence and a set of factors that constrain coherence.

Part 1. First, discuss the concepts and findings presented in the article:

1. What is instructional program coherence and how can it be achieved?
2. How does instructional program coherence promote student achievement?
3. The three schools in the study with the highest levels of instructional program coherence exhibited different means for achieving that coherence; two were democratic in their approach and one was autocratic. How do the authors describe the pros and cons of these two

different approaches to coherence? What insights do you have given your own experiences and your understanding of the change process?

Part 2. Second, apply the findings from Newmann and colleagues to the Sexton School District case. Discuss your interpretation in small groups.

4. In what ways do the Sexton School District and Carver Elementary exhibit instructional program coherence?
5. What factors facilitate instructional program coherence at Carver Elementary?
6. What are some of the constraints to instructional program coherence at Carver Elementary?

Step 4. Culminating Activity: Writing the Final Section of the Sexton Case Study

The culminating activity for this scaffolded case study is to write a concluding section to the Case of Sexton School District. Title your section *Part IV Instructional Improvement*. Focus on describing the influence of coaching on teachers' practice in years 2 and/or 3 of Math Investigations implementation. Be sure to include a description of:

1. Connie's work as the math coach. For example: functions, challenges, successes, etc.
2. The teachers' work. For example: interaction with one another, participation in grade level meetings, changes—if any—in practice, level of receptivity to Connie, etc.
3. Other relevant information. For example: parents, the math program, district context, administrators' roles, etc.

Your extension of the case should be approximately 2000 words and should follow, more or less, the style of the first three parts. Your part of the case will be entirely fictional, including any quotes you may decide to write.

Aurora School

PART ONE: SCHOOL CONTEXT AND THE NEED FOR REFORM

In this section of the case, you will read about the literacy reform undertaken by Aurora School. You will learn about the Aurora's cultural challenges, historically low achievement, and the resulting district intervention in the school.

Dr. Anita Soria's Lens

The school cafeteria was completely quiet. Forty-seven teachers stared at Dr. Anita Soria, the new board-appointed principal. "Good morning," Dr. Soria began. "Today, we begin our journey together. Today, we start the path to a new Aurora School. Today, we begin to change." She paused for a moment. Several teachers shifted nervously in their chairs, but the room remained quiet. "What do we need to work on in this school?" Dr. Soria asked. "I am new here. What are our strengths? What are our weaknesses?" Several teachers exchanged glances of surprise. After several more moments of silence, a teacher called out, "You are asking us?" "Yes," Dr. Soria responded, smiling slightly. "You know better than I do what needs to be done." Dr. Soria waited a few more moments. The silence was deafening in the room. "Okay, we need to get the conversation started. I want you to divide in grade-level groups. Each group will have chart paper, and markers. I want you to make two columns on your chart paper, one with strengths and the other with weaknesses. Assess Aurora. Then we will come back together and talk as a group again."

It was the week before the students would report back at Aurora and the first day teachers reported after a summer of turmoil. At the end of the previous school year, Aurora's principal of 10 years, Mr. Anderson, had been replaced by Dr. Soria by the board of education. It had been a difficult spring at Aurora, as there had been a large number of schools closed in the district. Staff at Aurora had felt certain that their school might be closed. Instead, the board had spared the school, at least to an extent. Rather than closing the school, district leadership had replaced the principal and mandated that the school adopt a required reading initiative and appoint a literacy coach who would work with teachers on the literacy materials.

128

Dr. Soria gave the Aurora teachers 20 minutes to compile their lists of school strengths and weaknesses. She circulated from group to group and listened to the conversations. As she did, she wrote notes to herself. "Fourth grade team is not talking," she wrote on her notepad. "How are we doing here?" she asked the teachers. "We don't know," one teacher responded. "Would you like a facilitator?" Dr. Soria asked. "No!" the teachers responded in unison. "Okay, then let's get going," Dr. Soria responded. Her voice sounded strong, but she felt her legs shaking as she walked to the next table where the third-grade teachers sat.

A strikingly different scene unfolded at the third-grade teachers' table. The teachers had already assembled a long list of strengths and had turned to the weaknesses. "Proud history. Cultural and ethnic diversity. Clean school. Orderly environment," the teachers had written under strengths. "The weaknesses list is difficult to write," one third-grade teacher stated, looking from her peers to Dr. Soria. "How can we be honest without offending anyone here?" she asked. "Honesty comes first," Dr. Soria responded. "Be honest and I will worry about managing the hard conversation," she continued to the teacher. The teacher looked skeptical but turned to the teacher who was writing the list. "Okay, then write 'Low expectations for students,'" she stated. Dr. Soria nodded and moved to the next group.

Later that evening, Dr. Soria sat in her new office with the chart papers arrayed around her and her notes from the meeting on her desk. The meeting had done exactly what she had hoped: it had given her a snapshot of the culture of the school. The fourth-grade teachers wrote only one strength and one weakness on their paper. The teachers had barely spoken to one another. Similarly, the first-grade teacher group had sat silently for most of the meeting. One teacher made the majority of the list without consulting with her colleagues in the final 2 minutes before the small-group time was over. The other grade levels could at least talk to each other, although the kind of conversations varied. The third-grade teachers seemed most enthusiastic about embracing change and improving the school. They had made a long list of weaknesses and had been thoughtful about providing some concrete ideas of improvement strategies during the whole-group discussion. The eighth-grade teachers had similarly generated a long list of weaknesses, but many of the weaknesses revolved around blaming the students for the poor performance of the school. "Students don't care, students have low achievement, students come from bad backgrounds," were the top three items on the eighth-grade teacher "weaknesses" list.

The whole-group discussion had a similar unevenness about it: some teachers did a lot of the talking while others did not speak at all, some teachers seemed to have a sense of concrete areas of improvement, while others wanted to talk only about the barriers to improving that they perceived as insurmountable.

Dr. Soria looked again at the achievement results from the school over the previous 5 years. It was a depressing situation at Aurora. Less than 20% of the school's students were at the national average in literacy. Only 21% were at that level in mathematics. The low achievement was in all grade levels, for the most part. There seemed to be some movement in third and sixth grade, but it appeared to be slight and inconsistent improvements that quickly disappeared in the grade levels that followed. As a school that served 900 K–8 students who were all low-income African American children in a large, urban district, the situation was desperate. Aurora needed to be doing a much better job educating the students, providing these children with a chance at academic success.

To Dr. Soria, the mandated literacy initiative was the perfect improvement strategy for a school like Aurora. A few years previously, the district had implemented an accountability system. Schools were sorted into categories based on their achievement. Schools where fewer than 15% of students were at national norms in reading were placed on probation. Even using this shockingly low standard, more than 100 schools were placed on probation in the first year of the accountability system. Some schools had improved and were able to move off probation. Others, like Aurora, had been on probation since the beginning of the accountability system. The bar had been slowly raised from 15% to 25%. Aurora could not keep up. "It is frustrating to me because we have improved," Mrs. Bardin, a fourth-grade teacher, stated at the meeting in the cafeteria. "Why do we still have to be on probation?" Dr. Soria shuddered as she remembered Mrs. Bardin's words. Did she not see that 15% was a low standard, that 25% was a low standard, that allowing 75 to 85% of children to be below the standard was unacceptable?

Mrs. Jesse Bardin's Lens

A few weeks later, Dr. Soria stood before the Aurora faculty again. "Welcome to the first in-service day," she stated. "Today we will learn about the literacy initiative we will undertake at Aurora. I see this as a tremendous opportunity for our school to improve. Today we will hear about the initiative from Dr. Margaret Smith, a literacy expert who was a part of one of the literacy teams that helped to design the initiative." There was scattered clapping as Dr. Smith walked to the center of the cafeteria. "The Literacy Framework is based around four cornerstones: Word Knowledge, Comprehension, Fluency, and Writing," Dr. Smith began. She spent the morning talking through each of the four foci of the initiative and the literacy activities that supported them. She described read-alouds, comprehension strategies, guided reading, and so on. She then handed out observation guides, rubrics that would be used to evaluate teacher performance on the various parts of the literacy initiative.

Mrs. Bardin's head spun as she listened to Dr. Smith. What were these people thinking? "Does anyone have any comments on the concept behind the framework?" Dr. Smith asked. There was a moment of silence and the teachers did not say anything. Mrs. Bardin hesitated but then decided to say out loud what she assumed other teachers were thinking. "The literacy practices you described seem sort of, shall we say, high-level for these kids," she stated slowly. "What do you mean?" asked Dr. Smith. "Say a bit more," she added. "I guess I just think about the students at Aurora, and I am not sure they can handle something like sustained collaborative discussion," Mrs. Bardin continued. "I can barely get them to complete the workbook activities after reading the textbook," she added.

Dr. Smith glanced at Principal Soria. Principal Soria raised her eyebrows. Mrs. Bardin felt herself growing angry. "You don't have to deal with the stuff that we deal with," she stated to Dr. Smith defiantly. "It is easy to sit at central office and plan this stuff in theory, but have you actually taught this stuff in a school like ours?" she asked. Dr. Smith continued the workshop without directly answering Mrs. Bardin's question. At lunch, Mrs. Bardin pointed that out to her grade-level colleague, Mrs. Ortiz. "She probably taught at some nice school with easy middle-class kids," Mrs. Bardin whispered to Mrs. Ortiz. Mrs. Ortiz nodded in agreement. "Shhhh," Mrs. Ortiz responded. "She is right over there."

Mrs. Bardin didn't care. She hoped that Dr. Smith and Dr. Soria had heard her. She was tired of the way that central office folks seemed to blame the teachers for the low achievement of kids like those at Aurora. She didn't think they understood what it was like to be a teacher in this context. Mrs. Bardin had been at Aurora for more than 15 years. The children in the school, she thought, were tough. She had been a seventh-grade teacher for most of her time at the school. The kids were hardly kids by the time they got to seventh grade. Mrs. Bardin had felt physically threatened plenty of times. These kids were out of control.

At the end of the in-service day, Principal Soria tapped Mrs. Bardin on the shoulder. "Could you stay after the session for a few minutes? Please come to my office," she stated. Mrs. Bardin knew that Dr. Soria was going to try to talk to her. That was okay; she had a few things to say to Dr. Soria, too.

Mrs. Bardin watched the second hand click on the clock as she waited for Dr. Soria. At last she arrived. "I only have a few minutes, I have to pick up my daughter soon," Mrs. Bardin told Dr. Soria. 'That is fine, this will only take a few minutes," Dr. Soria replied. "I was glad you were honest with Dr. Smith," Principal Soria began. "I think we are beginning to have some good, open conversations here at Aurora." Mrs. Bardin was surprised. "Yeah, I guess so," Mrs. Bardin mumbled in reply. "I actually want to talk to you about the literacy coach position. Do you remember Dr. Smith talking about it?" "Yes," Mrs. Bardin replied. Mrs. Bardin could not believe where the conversation was going. Could Dr. Soria really be asking her to take the literacy coach position? She thought the principal disliked her. Maybe the principal appreciated her after all! "I wanted you to know that I have offered the literacy coach position to Mrs. Santorini," Principal Soria stated slowly. "I wanted to tell you myself since I know you and she started at the school around the same time. I didn't want you to feel slighted." Mrs. Bardin deflated again. Dr. Soria didn't think she was any good. "Thanks for letting me know," Mrs. Bardin said briskly. "Will that be all?" Dr. Soria was quiet for a moment, as if she was deciding whether or not to say anything else. Before she could speak, Mrs. Bardin stormed out the door. So it was the same old thing after all.

PART TWO: THE FIRST PHASE OF THE LITERACY REFORM

In this section of the case, you will read about the first phase of the implementation of the literacy initiative. In particular, you will read about the work of the new literacy coach and her interpretation of the literacy framework.

Mrs. Delores Santorini's Lens

Delores Santorini stood at Principal Soria's door. It was the day of their first debriefing since Mrs. Santorini had been named Aurora's literacy coach. "What are we talking about today?" Mrs. Santorini asked the principal. "I was hoping you could give me an update on the observations you did in teachers' classrooms," Dr. Soria stated. "And then perhaps we can strategize about how to move the literacy work forward." Mrs. Santorini opened her folder, which contained the observations she had undertaken. "There is something else I was hoping we could discuss," Mrs. Santorini began. "What is it?" asked Principal Soria. "It is the literacy framework. I think it is ambitious for our teachers and our students," Mrs. Santorini explained. "I would like to suggest a modified version of the framework."

For Mrs. Santorini, the transition to literacy coach had not been easy. It was not that she didn't have the experience; she had been a classroom teacher for more than 15 years. It also was not that she didn't have the rapport necessary to work with the teachers at Aurora. For the most part, she got along with everyone at the school and they had been relatively open to her visits. It was the framework. She didn't agree with it. When Mrs. Bardin had spoken out at the professional development session, she had silently agreed. "I don't think these activities are appropriate for Aurora's students," she explained to Dr. Soria. "We need basic skills here and tightly controlled discipline."

In the first phase of her work, Mrs. Santorini had observed most of the teachers' classrooms. She had used the observation guide provided by the district. What she saw was that most teachers were not using the literacy framework activities. When they found out she was coming to observe, many tried to use some of the activities. However, they were attempting to integrate them into the existing reading textbooks they were using. The small-group components of the literacy framework were largely not being used. For example, the literacy framework described guided reading, a strategy that relied upon small-group work. Only one of Aurora's teachers had attempted this practice. When Mrs. Santorini asked Mrs. Mandela why she hadn't used it, Mrs. Mandela responded, "What are the rest of my students going to do while I work in small groups? There is no way my students are mature enough to occupy themselves." She told Mrs. Santorini that instead of guided reading she was having the students do choral reading, in which the students read out loud as a class. "I can circulate as the students are reading and make corrections as they read," she explained. "But I don't have to worry about the management nightmare of small-group work."

A different issue with the same kind of result occurred in Ms. Elle's second-grade class. "The level of writing that this framework assumes for second-grade students is ridiculous," Ms. Elle told Mrs. Santorini. "I think the worksheets that I use to have my students fill in details after a provided topic sentence makes much more sense for the kids at this school." Mrs. Santorini told Ms. Elle that she would talk more to the regional literacy coach about this approach. "Perhaps we can see if this could be an approved substitute for the district approach," she told Ms. Elle.

Mrs. Santorini was torn about how to respond to comments like this. On the one hand, she knew that her new role was intended to support the implementation of the practices within the literacy initiative. On the other hand, she felt fairly certain that if she were still a teacher being pushed to implement these practices, she would feel much the same way that Mrs. Mandela and Ms. Elle felt.

In her meeting with Dr. Soria, Mrs. Santorini began to describe the conversations she had with teachers. "Their requests for modification of the framework really do seem reasonable," she told Dr. Soria.

Mrs. Holly Alameda's Lens

Mrs. Alameda was the regional literacy coach. "I think we have a problem with your literacy coach," she told Principal Soria. "She seems to think that the literacy framework is optional." Principal Soria sighed. "I know," she replied. "I am just not sure what to do about it." Dr. Soria closed her office door. She explained to Mrs. Alameda her decision to select Mrs. Santorini. "I knew she was not as innovative as I might like," she stated. "But I also knew that in a school like Aurora, seniority was a key issue. I felt if I selected someone more junior or someone from the outside the teachers would not work with the person," she continued. "While that may be true, she is not pushing the teachers to change their practice," Mrs. Alameda replied. "What can we do about this?"

Mrs. Alameda emerged from the meeting with Principal Soria full of questions. She hoped she had made it clear to Principal Soria that if Mrs. Santorini could not deepen her work and be convinced to push teachers in the direction of using the literacy framework, she would have to be replaced. The situation at Aurora was much like that of several schools in her region that were under her charge. The schools' literacy coaches were not on board with the literacy framework, did not have the skills to lead teachers to improve, or lacked the relationships with teachers to do the work. Mrs. Alameda sighed. She would have to take them one school, one situation at a time. It was her job to push each school to improve, whatever it took.

Mentally, she prepared herself for the difficult conversation at Aurora that lay ahead. On Tuesday she would meet with Principal Soria and Mrs. Santorini during their weekly chat. She had agreed with Dr. Soria that it was best that the principal take the lead in the conversation with Mrs. Santorini. She would just be there to provide support and observe. "I do not intend to intervene in the conversation," she told Dr. Soria the next Tuesday morning as the pair prepared for the conversation with Mrs. Santorini. "This is your show. I am just here to support you." Principal Soria nodded. "I appreciate you being here," she stated. "If you want me to do or say anything, however, just let me know," Mrs. Alameda added.

A few minutes later, Mrs. Santorini arrived in the principal's office for the weekly chat with Dr. Soria. She saw Mrs. Alameda as she entered the office and looked surprised. Mrs. Alameda realized that Principal Soria had not informed Mrs. Santorini that she would be at the meeting. Mrs. Alameda wondered if that had been a good decision. Perhaps she should have encouraged Dr. Soria to tell Mrs. Santorini that she would be there. Mrs. Alameda shook these thoughts from her head. No reason to think about this now. She refocused on the conversation that Dr. Soria and Mrs. Santorini were having.

"What I am saying is that we are being judged on this framework and so we have to push our teachers to use it," Principal Soria stated. "I understand that," Mrs. Santorini stated. "But what can I do if I don't believe in it myself? And how do I push the teachers? They are my colleagues, my friends. I have no real power over them, nor do I want it." The conversation grew increasingly tense as the principal and the literacy coach continued to talk.

"Why did you offer me this position to begin with?" Mrs. Santorini finally stated. "I was much better at just being a teacher. I never should have tried to take on this role." Principal Soria sighed and looked at Mrs. Alameda. Mrs. Alameda realized that Principal Soria couldn't argue with Mrs. Santorini. The principal had chosen Mrs. Santorini to fill the literacy coach position based on seniority rather than based on level of innovation. "I had to choose between a teacher who would be more easily accepted and trusted at a place like Aurora where issues of territory and trust were difficult and one who might bring more innovative ways of thinking," she explained to Mrs. Alameda after Mrs. Santorini left. "Did I make the wrong choice?" Mrs. Alameda thought for a moment before responding. "You did the best you could under the circumstances," she stated. "There is no reason to beat yourself up about it."

A month later, Principal Soria, Mrs. Alameda, and Mrs. Santorini sat again at the table in the principal's office facing one another. "Let's talk through the fourth-grade teachers' progress together," Mrs. Alameda suggested. Mrs. Santorini looked at Principal Soria. She didn't speak for a moment. "They are at about the same place they were the last time we talked," she told Dr. Soria. "Have you been able to push them on their use of the guided reading practices?" Dr. Soria asked. Mrs. Alameda held her breath as Mrs. Santorini slowly considered her response. "No, I haven't," she finally responded. "I think it is time that I step down as literacy coach," she stated, looking at Principal Soria. "I don't believe in what I am doing." Principal Soria nodded. "It seems like this is the best decision." Mrs. Alameda also nodded. The conversation with Mrs. Santorini continued for a few minutes more as she explained in further detail her decision. Mrs. Alameda's mind wandered. Who might fill the literacy coach position at Aurora?

Late into the evening after Mrs. Santorini left, Principal Soria and Mrs. Alameda talked through replacement options for the literacy coach position. "Do you have any other options on your staff?" Mrs. Alameda asked. The two discussed a third-grade teacher, Ms. Tamerin, for a few minutes. "Yes, she is innovative, but she is so young," Principal Soria stated. "And a lot of the teachers are really put off by her over-the-top, energetic, optimistic disposition," Dr. Soria continued. "She is wonderful to me, but I think she is a walking nightmare to some of the more senior teachers," she stated. Dr. Soria and Mrs. Alameda looked at each other for a moment and then burst into laughter. "This is impossible to get right, isn't it?" Mrs. Alameda asked. "Without a doubt. I feel like I am in a no-win situation," Dr. Soria responded.

Through two additional meetings, Mrs. Alameda and Dr. Soria debated the merits of a variety of candidates, both internal and external to the school. In the end, they decided to interview two external candidates for the position. "Perhaps an insider perspective is just the wrong perspective in this case," Mrs. Alameda told Principal Soria. "Let's find a good, innovative, enthusiastic outsider to come in and shake things up." Dr. Soria agreed. "Preferably someone with thick skin."

A New Beginning

"Alicia Brown, nice to meet you," the candidate for the literacy coach position stated as she extended her hand to Mrs. Bardin. Mrs. Bardin did not speak, just nodded and shook the candidate's hand. Mrs. Alameda wondered how this would go. Mrs. Santorini had stepped down as literacy coach and Dr. Soria had decided to bring in two outsiders to be considered for the position. As a representative on the Leadership Committee, Mrs. Bardin was one of the staff people who would have a say in selecting Mrs. Santorini's replacement. Mrs. Alameda knew that Mrs. Bardin had felt resentment at being overlooked for the literacy coach position and that she had been a vocal resistor to the implementation of the literacy framework. As Mrs. Brown was introduced to the selection committee, Mrs. Alameda looked over the candidate's résumé again. Northwestern University. Harvard. Literacy coach at central office. Alicia Brown had an amazing set of credentials. It was Mrs. Bardin's turn to ask a question. Mrs. Alameda looked up. What would Mrs. Bardin say? "Have you ever worked with kids like ours?" Mrs. Bardin asked. Mrs. Alameda cringed and glanced around. She saw Principal Soria's mouth curved into a frown. All eyes looked at Mrs. Brown. "What do you mean, 'kids like ours'?" Alicia responded quickly. "Kids from tough backgrounds, kids with drugs in their lives, kids in gangs," Mrs. Bardin responded. "I think I was a kid like that," Alicia responded. "I grew up less than a mile from here." Mrs. Bardin didn't ask any more questions. As the rest of the selection committee excitedly asked questions, it was clear to Mrs. Alameda that Alicia Brown's term as literacy coach at Aurora was about to begin.

PART THREE: THE SECOND PHASE
OF THE LITERACY REFORM

In this section of the case, you will read about the second phase of the implementation of the literacy initiative at Aurora. In particular, you will read about the work of Alicia Brown, the literacy coach who replaced Mrs. Santorini, and the teacher resistance and isolation she faced in her role.

Dr. Anita Soria's Lens

Alicia Brown stood tall in the front of the cafeteria. "Hello!" she called out to the teachers. There were a few mumbled responses. Most teachers looked at the floor. "I said, HELLO," she yelled, smiling and jumping up and down. Principal Soria laughed, as did a few other teachers. It was hard not to like Alicia Brown. She was an energetic, enthusiastic person. "I am not afraid to look like a fool if it helps to make the teachers feel comfortable," she told Principal Soria immediately before the meeting began. Dr. Soria could see that she wasn't kidding.

Mrs. Brown stood in front of the teachers waving a stack of papers. "This is our new plan," she stated. "I am going to start observations and demonstrations in your classrooms. It is time we get to know these literacy framework practices." She handed the stack to several teachers, who began to hand them around. On it was a schedule of visitations and demonstrations in different teachers' classrooms. "Mark your calendars, I am coming, ready or not!" she yelled. A few more teachers chuckled. "She is so crazy," one teacher muttered to the colleague sitting next to her. "I sure am," Alicia smiled, overhearing. "Crazy about literacy!" Groans echoed throughout the cafeteria, but most teachers smiled.

After the meeting with the teachers, Dr. Soria and Alicia Brown met in the principal's office. The pair discussed the observation and demonstration schedule. "I am surprised you decided to go to Mrs. Bardin's classroom so early in your schedule," Principal Soria commented. "You know she is one of the biggest resistors to the literacy work." Mrs. Brown nodded. "That is exactly why I put her in the first group of teachers," she responded. "I want to send a message that we are going to push on those who are not moving. I put all of the most resistant teachers first." Dr. Soria felt skeptical but she simply nodded and asked, "Are you ready to fight those battles?" Alicia smiled. "I am ready if you are!"

Mrs. Jesse Bardin's Lens

A few days later, Alicia stood in front of Mrs. Bardin's classroom. "Today, we are going to start on a writing project that is going to last for the next two weeks," Mrs. Brown told the class. "We will work to produce a piece of writing of which you can be proud. You will read it and share it with some of your classmates." Alicia began to walk the students through the writing process. She handed out a sample of writing. "I want you to take a few minutes to read this," she told the students. "It is a positive example of the kind of writing I am talking about. Read it silently. You will then meet in partners and discuss what makes this a positive example."

Mrs. Bardin sat in the back, feeling skeptical. Before the lesson began, she and Alicia had previewed the lesson together. "My students will not sit still to do this reading," Mrs. Bardin commented. "And I am not sure they can have the level of discussion you are looking for in the partnering." Alicia had simply nodded. "Let's just see how it goes today," she responded. "After the lesson, let's talk again and we can discuss what I need to tweak for the lesson tomorrow, all right?" Mrs. Bardin had nodded in return, but in her head she felt certain that this lesson was going to be a disaster. What Mrs. Brown was proposing was so different from anything her students had ever done. How would they respond?

Mrs. Bardin was surprised to see that most of the students were completing the assigned reading of the model student writing. Mrs. Brown had asked the students to take notes as they read, writing down the aspects of the example that made it an exemplar. Several students were actually doing that. Mrs. Brown had also asked the students to raise their hands if there were words they did not know in the writing sample. A few minutes passed and two different students raised their hands. Mrs. Brown approached each and quietly told the students the words with which they were not familiar. One student, a stocky boy named Joseph Avalon, began kicking the chair of the student in front of him. "Stop it!" the boy stage-whispered to Joseph. "I ain't doing nothin,'" Joseph responded loudly. Mrs. Bardin immediately was on edge, ready to pounce. "Here we go," she thought to herself. She imagined the lesson unraveling and imagined how long it would take to get student discipline under control again after this lesson. Mrs. Bardin made a move to walk over to Joseph. As she did, Alicia held up her hand, motioning for Mrs. Bardin to wait. Mrs. Brown approached Joseph and whispered something to him, her hand on his shoulder. He whispered something back. Mrs. Brown responded. Joseph looked at her and then began to read the assignment again. Mrs. Bardin sat back in her chair and felt a new respect for Mrs. Brown. Maybe she could handle the class after all.

Most of the students had completed reading the exemplar. Mrs. Brown held up her hand. "So I want to tell you one thing about this piece of writing before we get into partners to discuss the strengths of it," she told the students. "Joseph and I were just discussing it, actually," she stated motioning to the student. "Joseph, can you tell me who wrote this piece?" "Yeah, she said it came from a student at Bayfield." There were audible gasps in the room. Bayfield was the elementary school down the street from Aurora and the sworn enemy in sports, particularly in basketball. "Who won the last Bayfield–Aurora basketball game?" Mrs. Brown asked. "We won, we won!" several students called out. "Well, now you need to work on being this good in writing," Mrs. Brown responded. "If they can do it, so can you!" Mrs. Bardin found herself smiling. Using Bayfield was a very good idea. She looked at Mrs. Brown and saw that she was smiling, too.

Mrs. Bardin and Mrs. Brown sat at a table with Dr. Soria. It was several weeks later and the demonstration writing unit was over in Mrs. Bardin's class. "Well, how did it go?" asked Dr. Soria. Mrs. Bardin looked at Mrs.

Brown, anxious to hear what she had to say. How did the literacy coach perceive that this had gone? Mrs. Brown didn't speak, however, but instead nodded at Mrs. Bardin to respond. "What do you think, Jesse?" she asked. Mrs. Bardin was surprised that Mrs. Brown was allowing her to answer the question. She hesitated for a moment. "I guess I was surprised at what the students wrote. They did better than I thought they would," she admitted. As she said it, she realized that it was actually true. Mrs. Brown had demonstrated that the literacy activities worked with her students. They were engaged and excited, and they had produced writing that was far beyond Mrs. Bardin's expectations. Mrs. Bardin noticed that Dr. Soria and Mrs. Brown exchanged smiles. And she didn't even mind.

Alicia Brown's Lens

The early success with Mrs. Bardin raised Alicia Brown's spirits. "We are on a roll," she told Principal Soria. "Imagine what we can do if we turn other resistant teachers!" She went home after the meeting with Mrs. Bardin feeling energized and excited. This was the reason she had taken this role in such a difficult school! Alicia thought back on that day many times in the weeks that followed. She had purposely front-loaded her observation and demonstration schedule with the most resistant teachers at Aurora. And it was becoming apparent that not all of the resistant teachers would come on board in the manner that Mrs. Bardin had. Teachers put Alicia off, turned her away, refused to talk to her in the hallways or lunchroom. Mrs. Brown continued to carry herself in her usual cheery manner, but the difficulty of the work began to wear on her. "I am struggling," she confided in Dr. Soria one evening as the two happened to be leaving the school at 8:00 P.M. "So many teachers seem to think that I am the enemy. So many teachers think the students in this school can't do the simplest tasks. I feel like I am not making progress!" The words spilled out. Alicia felt tears streaming down her face. Dr. Soria took Mrs. Brown by the arm and led her to her car. "Get in," she told Mrs. Brown. After a time, Mrs. Brown finally stopped crying and took a breath. "Do you have time to get some dinner?" Dr. Soria asked. Mrs. Brown nodded. "Okay, the rule is, though, for the first thirty minutes we talk no work, all right?" Mrs. Brown agreed enthusiastically, "Okay!" As the pair drove to a nearby restaurant, Alicia already felt better. Thank goodness for Anita Soria. She would have quit many times without this positive relationship with Aurora's principal.

Two hours later, the pair stopped their social conversation and returned to the topic of instruction at Aurora. "Alicia, I think your focus on these toughest teachers is admirable. But you are driving yourself crazy. It is time to work with a few more enthusiastic teachers." Mrs. Brown hesitated. She had explicitly organized her schedule this way in order to push the resistors. Was she giving up? A few minutes passed before she finally spoke. "You are right," Alicia stated, sighing. "I wish that working with these resistant teachers was working, but it is killing me to have so little success," she continued. The two worked through Alicia's schedule, distributing the remainder of the resistant teachers across several weeks. "It will be good to feel successful again," Alicia sighed. She drove home feeling better. Tomorrow was another day.

The end of the year was approaching and Mrs. Brown and Dr. Soria sat together with the roster of teachers at Aurora before them. "What do you think about Noreen?" Principal Soria asked. Alicia sighed. "She has continued to resist. She acted so on board during the demonstration. When I dropped in a few weeks ago, nothing looked different in her classroom. The students were doing worksheets." Principal Soria added the teacher to the growing list of those who were still not implementing the literacy framework. "That makes eighteen teachers who still haven't started using the literacy framework in any meaningful way," Dr. Soria stated. "Not bad, not bad," Alicia stated encouragingly. "We have made progress. " "Not enough, I don't think," Dr. Soria stated. "But there is Mrs. Bardin," Principal Soria added. It was true. All along, Mrs. Brown had thought that Mrs. Bardin would be the biggest resistor. Because she was so vocal in her resistance, Alicia and Dr. Soria believed she would never come on board. It turned out, however, that Mrs. Bardin had become a strong supporter of the literacy framework. It was the silent resistors who were turning out to be the biggest barriers to uniform implementation in the school. "Look at this list," Mrs. Brown stated, shaking her head. "Many of these teachers I never would have guessed would be so difficult to push. What a shock." "I was just thinking the same thing," responded Dr. Soria. "Okay, what now?" Alicia thought for a moment. "Why don't I take some time to think of next steps and strategies and then we can talk about it next week?" Dr. Soria agreed.

Alicia thought about possible next steps. She reflected upon her work across the year. Alicia had spent her 1st year visiting classrooms. She had completed demonstration lessons in all teachers' classrooms at Aurora. In the classrooms of teachers whom Mrs. Brown perceived were most resistant to the literacy framework, she had done extended lessons. In the classrooms of teachers who seemed to be on board, she had spent less time, a class period or a portion of a class period. The demonstration lesson cycle had taken most of the year. Mrs. Brown and Dr. Soria followed this intensive demonstration cycle with an intensive observation cycle. The pair conducted drop-in visits to all the teachers together. Alicia looked over the observation notes she and Dr. Soria had taken. She used them to make a list of teachers who were moving and not moving based on the observations.

A week later, Mrs. Brown and Dr. Soria sat together and considered the list. The resistant teachers were spread across most grade levels. However, more of the teachers were clustered in the middle grades, four through six, where 12 of the teachers were located. "I think some mandatory professional development by grade area is just what we need," Dr. Soria said thoughtfully. "Let's target these teachers and really push them as a group." Mrs. Brown agreed. "I think that is a great idea," she responded. As the pair worked out the details of the professional development plan, Alicia again felt fortunate that she and Dr. Soria had such a good working relationship. She felt sure that this difficult work would be impossible without her support.

One Step, One Day at a Time

Alicia Brown stood before the fourth-, fifth-, and sixth-grade teachers. It was 7:00 A.M. on the first Wednesday of school. All the teachers who had signed up for the session were in attendance. "Let's get started, our time is short," Mrs. Brown stated cheerfully.

The mandatory professional development seemed to be working to make some changes. Four of the teachers left over the summer when they were told by Dr. Soria that they would have to attend professional development on the literacy framework. "Your time will be paid if you choose to attend outside of school hours," Dr. Soria told the teachers. "But you must attend, either before school, after school, or during school with a substitute in your classroom."

The eight remaining teachers, along with the teachers hired to replace those who had chosen to leave, sat in the library listening to Mrs. Brown. There was a quiet murmur in the library as the teachers worked in pairs and trios in their grade levels to design a literature circle activity that they would then use in their classrooms in the coming week. Mrs. Brown had purposely grouped the new teachers with the experienced teachers. "How about we try a different book?" Mrs. Brown heard Ms. Amos, a new teacher, ask one of the veterans. "I worry students will be so bored with the readings you suggest from the textbook." The veteran teacher reluctantly agreed, and the group moved on together to identify a new reading. Alicia Brown smiled to herself. Integrating the new teachers into the veteran teacher groups was working beautifully. The new teachers were pushing the status quo, and the veteran teachers were stepping up to mentor.

A year later, Alicia and Principal Soria took stock again. The list of resistant teachers was down to 3. Between professional development, changed teacher perceptions, and teachers leaving, the implementation of the framework was moving along. Principal Soria remained concerned. "Why can't we see it in the test scores, that really worries me," Dr. Soria confided to

Alicia. The achievement scores had crept up slightly, but the pattern only mirrored state and district averages. Aurora was not making gains that were significantly different from other schools in the district. "It will come, it will come," Alicia responded. The signs were present that real change was happening. Teacher conversations were different. Student conversations were different. Classroom climate was different. Alicia felt confident that the test scores would follow if the school just stayed true to the path they were on. "I hope you are right," Dr. Soria responded. The next round of school closings is about to come out and I just pray that we are not on it."

Aurora Teaching Notes

ACTIVITY. CASE ANALYSIS

Objective: To analyze the case of Aurora School using literature on scaling up reform and a previous analytical lens. Our analysis will include four steps:

1. Establish the facts of the case.
2. Analyze the case using literature on scaling up reform.
3. Analyze the case using a previous analytical lens.
4. Write a memo to Principal Soria as a culminating activity.

Each of these steps is elaborated below.

Step 1. Establishing the Facts of the Case

Begin by recalling the facts of the case, using Table 3.5 in the Appendix as a guide. This process will help you establish what is known and unknown about the case. Be careful to distinguish between known facts and presumptions.

Further solidify your understanding of the case by comparing your list of facts with a partner. Clarify and reconcile any areas of disagreement or inconsistency. When you feel confident that you know the facts of the case, proceed to Step 2.

Step 2. Analysis: Scaling Up Reform

The second step in analyzing the case of Aurora School is to consider the change process underlying the reforms that are taking place. Read the article by Fullan (2000) and complete the activities below.

Reading 1

Fullan, M. (2000). The three stories of education reform. *Phi Delta Kappan,*
 81(8), 581–584.

In *"The Three Stories of Education Reform,"* Michael Fullan summarizes three
dimensions of school reform: the inside story (internal school dynamics), the
inside–outside story (external forces influencing the school), and the outside-
in story (external agencies organizing to improve schools). Fullan emphasizes
the importance of understanding and coordinating these three layers in and
around schools to successfully scale up school reform initiatives.

Part 1. In this activity, you will focus on the "inside story." Fullan finds
that "the existence of collaborative work cultures (or professional learning communities) makes a difference in how well students do in school"
(p. 582). Summarizing the work of Newmann and Wehlage, Fullan suggests that successful schools: (1) form professional learning communities,
(2) focus on student work (assessment), and (3) change their instructional
practice in accordance with assessment to improve results (p. 582). In small
groups, discuss Aurora in relationship to these three dimensions of successful
schools.

1. In what ways has Aurora been successful with regard to these
   dimensions?
2. What challenges does the school have?

Part 2. In this activity, you will focus on the "inside-out story." In small
groups, discuss the external factors that might influence the process of school
improvement at Aurora. What external people or organizations might serve
as supports for the "inside story" you discussed in Part 1?

Step 3. Analysis: Revisiting a Previous Analytical Lens

This book has introduced a variety of lenses for case analysis. Analyze the
case of Aurora using one of these previously applied lenses. Choose one of
the following four lenses: (1) professional communities (Part 2, Open-Ended
Case 2), (2) social and relational trust (Part 2, Open-Ended Case 3), (3) the
change process (Part 3, Barley School), or (4) instructional program coherence (Part 3, Sexton School District).

Part 1. Apply the lens you have chosen to the case of Aurora. What does
the analytical lens tell us about the case? Note whatever implications the lens
you applied suggests for promoting improvement at Aurora.

Part 2. Pair with another student who applied a different analytical lens than the one you chose. Share the application of your lens (in Activity 3) with each other. What different insights does each lens offer?

Step 4. Culminating Activity: A Memo to Principal Soria

Write a brief memo (2–3 pages) to Principal Soria suggesting an avenue for improving the inside story at Aurora. In your memo, draw upon your knowledge of scaling up in Step 2 and the analytical lens you applied in Step 3.

Drawing Conclusions from the Cases:
Themes and Future Inquiry

A group of principals sat in a district professional development session. They were there to learn more about the reading initiative that would begin in their buildings when school opened in a few days. A small portion of the half-day session was devoted to discussing the work of the school-level literacy coaches who would work as instructional teacher leaders in their schools. A district-level literacy coach made a presentation about the work of the school-level literacy coach. She led the principals in small-group activities where they discussed the role functions of the coaches, the challenges the coaches might encounter in building relationships of trust with teachers, and the ways in which the principal might support and work with their coach. At the end of the session the presenter asked the principals, "Do you have any questions about the work of your literacy coaches?" One principal raised her hand. "How do we know if the coaches work?" she asked. "What do you mean?" replied the district literacy coach. "I guess what I mean is, what is the measure of success for these positions?" the principal asked.

The work we have undertaken in this volume contributes to an emergent literature that aims to define, clarify, and deepen understanding of the functions, challenges, and contexts of instructional teacher leaders. We have told the stories of instructional teacher leaders, using their experiences and words to help define what they do and how they do it. We have used research to frame the dilemmas that teacher leaders face and applied analytical lenses to think through ways to manage those challenges. We have situated the stories of teacher leaders within the complex contexts in which they work: neighborhoods, districts, reform initiatives, school cultures, and individual perspectives. While this volume has offered many ways to think about instructional teacher leaders, questions remain. In this concluding chapter we consider some of the themes that run through the cases and identify pressing questions that are yet to be answered in future inquiry.

CONSIDERING THEMES AND DEFINING AREAS OF FUTURE INQUIRY

In this section we discuss five underexamined themes in need of further investigation: (1) the level of structure associated with the instructional teacher leader role and related curriculum and reforms; (2) the extent to which interaction with the instructional teacher leader and implementation of related reforms is mandated; (3) the relationship among evaluation, supervision, and instructional teacher leadership; (4) the need for more information about the work of secondary-level instructional teacher leader roles; and, finally, (5) the potential differences in instructional teacher leader enactment associated with different subject areas.

Level of Structure

One variation across the case studies is the extent to which instructional teacher leader roles are structured and the structure of the initiatives and curriculum within which these roles are implemented. In some of the cases, the instructional teacher leader works within the context of a prescriptive reform with clearly delineated functions and tasks. For example, the case of Stella (Part 1, Vignette 3) illustrates how a highly defined literacy facilitator role operates within a tightly structured curriculum and reform initiative, Success for All. Like some other comprehensive reform models, Success for All contains a framework for the literacy facilitator position that provides a clear focus for her work and specific functions to be enacted.

In contrast, Matt, a math coordinator (Part 1, Vignette 2), worked with the district-level curriculum specialist to design his role. Unlike Stella, he was not bound to a particular model of instructional teacher leadership and was not required to engage in specific functions or tasks. Matt and his supervisor designed the role to facilitate teacher collaboration so that teachers might "support one another in the implementation of the new math program." Beyond the need to implement the new math program, Matt and the supervisor were free to design the role as they saw fit. The high level of discretion afforded to Matt allowed him to be flexible in how he worked with individual teachers, tailoring support to their individual needs.

It is unclear how the level of structure associated with instructional teacher leader roles influences their work. The culture of schools has long resisted efforts to reduce teachers' autonomy and standardize instructional practices (Lortie, 1975). At the same time, clear guidelines, protocols, and professional development activities aimed at showing teachers how to change their practice have been shown to prompt real changes in teachers' instruction (Cohen & Hill, 2001). To what extent might these findings translate to the work of instructional teacher leaders? Might highly structured roles reduce ambiguity and facilitate change? Might less structured roles allow for flexibility and responsiveness to individual teachers' needs?

Paradoxically, evidence from the cases in this volume suggests that both may be true. Stella, the instructional teacher leader who worked as a Success for All literacy facilitator, positively interpreted her highly structured role: "Using the SFA program makes it much easier to define the parameters of my role. The structured nature of the approach makes my role clear." In the case of Matt, his less structured and more flexible role allowed him to differentiate his work based on teachers' needs. Rather than being forced into a highly scripted role, he had greater autonomy and discretion over the enactment of his role.

The idea that both highly structured and less structured roles have benefits raises the question of which design to implement under what conditions. Could it be that each design is best suited for different kinds of contexts? Additional inquiry is needed to better understand how the level of structure interacts with the school context to influence the effectiveness of instructional teacher leader roles.

Mandatory or Voluntary Reforms

Closely related to the level of structure surrounding instructional teacher leader roles is the extent to which the work associated with these roles is mandatory or voluntary. Specifically, the cases in this volume illustrate variations in (1) the extent to which instructional practices were mandated, (2) the extent to which interaction with the coach is mandated, and, relatedly, (3) the level of control and oversight applied to the enactment of the instructional teacher leader role.

The case of Aurora School (Part 3, scaffolded case 3) illustrates a district-mandated reform for low-performing schools. In association with the mandated reform, Aurora was assigned a board-appointed principal and instructed to implement a prescribed approach to literacy instruction. In contrast, the Barley School case (Part 3, scaffolded case 1) portrays a voluntary approach to reform undertaken by a principal trying to improve instructional practices in literacy. Principal Stillman joined a network of schools committed to implementing a literacy framework with the support of a university partner.

This variation in the extent to which instructional practices are mandatory or voluntary has implications for the implementation of the instructional teacher leader role, affecting the degree to which interaction with the teacher leader is mandatory or voluntary. At Aurora, Principal Soria and literacy coach Alicia Brown made teacher participation in professional development around the literacy initiative mandatory. Alicia scheduled demonstration and observations in all teachers' classrooms, and teachers who were identified as being resistant to the literacy framework practices or in need of further training were required to attend additional professional development. Similarly, Principal Malen required teachers to work with Jeff, the math lead at

Portland Elementary (Part 2, Open-Ended Case 4) at least twice during the year. In addition, she indicated to teachers that their instruction in math would be considered in their formal evaluation.

In a contrasting example, MaryAnn (Part 2, Open-Ended Case 3), whose work with the teachers in her school was voluntary, found that she worked closely with only about 25% of the teachers. Although MaryAnn wanted to work with more teachers, interactions were not mandated, leaving it up to teachers to decide the extent to which they would work with MaryAnn and implement changes to their instruction. While Emily Chalmers, the district-level literacy coach, told MaryAnn she should "pressure teachers to be on board," the case is left open for students to discuss the pros and cons of using threats to leverage access to classrooms.

The extent to which interaction with the instructional teacher leader is mandatory or voluntary also has implications for the level of accountability and oversight of the teacher leader role itself. In some cases, the instructional teacher leader's work may be closely monitored. One example of this was Tara, a literacy coach (Part 1, Vignette 9) whose work was supported and overseen by district-level literacy coaches. In this vignette, Dr. Ortega was responsible for "coaching the coaches" and, if necessary, influencing the enactment of the school-level literacy coach role. In the words of Dr. Ortega, "I see Tara as needing to undertake more co-teaching and demonstration in the classroom. It is part of my role to mold her approach to her work, in ways that I think will benefit her school." In instances where instructional teacher leaders are closely monitored, supervisors may review both the teacher leader's work as well as the level of instructional improvement occurring in classrooms.

The level of oversight evident in the vignette with Tara is markedly different from Jeff's experiences at Westin and Portland Elementary Schools (Part 2, Open-Ended Case 4). Absent a mandatory reform program to implement, Jeff's role was to support teachers' development of math content knowledge and instructional improvement. While the principals at each of the buildings where he worked were responsible for overseeing his work, they exhibited drastically different approaches. Principal Weaver took a hands-off approach, seldom inquiring into Jeff's work or his progress with instructional improvement. On the other hand, Principal Malen offered a high level of monitoring and guidance, supporting Jeff in the implementation of his role by pressuring teachers to improve and signaling Jeff as a key resource. In this example, lack of a mandated reform model, program, or curriculum did not preclude the supervisor from actively monitoring and supporting the work of instructional teacher leadership.

One way to conceptualize the mandatory/voluntary nature of reform is to view reform strategies along a continuum of greater and lesser commitment and control (Rowan, 1990). Rowan describes control-oriented strategies as "increasing bureaucratic controls over curriculum and teaching" (p. 353). On the other hand, commitment-oriented strategies involve "a decrease in bureaucratic controls in education and the creation of working conditions in schools that enhance the commitment and expertise of teachers" (p. 353). The cases in this volume illustrate the use of both control and commitment strategies, at times in the same reform approach. Schools and districts strive to balance carrots and sticks; structure and autonomy; control and commitment.

In some instances school districts are moving toward portfolio strategies to reform education (Hill, 2006; Hill, Campbell, & Harvey, 2000) that involve multiple reform initiatives with different levels of control and commitment depending on the perceived needs of the school. For instance, the mandatory literacy initiative described in the Aurora School case (Part 3, scaffolded case 3) was implemented for low-achieving schools, while high-achieving schools in the same district were part of an initiative that gave them increased autonomy. Again, this suggests that the context for instructional teacher leadership initiatives influences its design—in this case, the extent to which interaction with the role and its related reforms are mandatory or voluntary.

The influence of mandatory versus voluntary reforms on instructional teacher leadership is unclear from the cases in this volume. Deeper investigation is necessary to determine whether a mandatory reform initiative leads to clearer definition of the instructional teacher leader role. Does an optional reform lead to higher levels of teacher buy-in?

Evaluation and Supervision

Closely associated with the issues discussed in the previous section is the question of whether or not the instructional teacher leader should play a role in overseeing and/or evaluating the classroom teacher. The cases of instructional teacher leadership we have highlighted in this book portray roles that are nonsupervisory in nature. In previous work we have argued that the nonsupervisory nature of the instructional teacher leader role is critical to developing relationships of trust (Mangin & Stoelinga, 2008, p. 189). Yet it should be noted that nonsupervisory is not synonymous with nonevaluative. The instructional teacher leaders in the cases in this volume were responsible for working to help teachers evaluate their practice and determine areas for improvement. This kind of supportive evaluation process is distinct from the supervisory evaluation conducted by principals, whose job is to evaluate teachers' instruction for the purpose of determining performance based promotions or sanctions.

At the same time, the world of teacher evaluation is in flux. Principals are increasingly encouraged to act not merely as performance evaluators but to serve as instructional leaders, providing support to teachers. And in some cases, principals ask instructional teacher leaders to conduct supervisory-style evaluations or provide evaluative feedback to principals on the progress that teachers make in their instructional improvement efforts. These practices may be especially prevalent in the context of highly structured and/or mandatory reforms. Typically, in the practitioner-oriented literature, such practices are considered antithetical to effective teacher leader practice insofar as they are perceived as diminishing trust between the teacher leader and the classroom teacher. To date, we know of no direct investigations that compare nonsupervisory instructional teacher leader roles to roles with a supervisory component.

The question of whether or not instructional teacher leaders should play a supervisory role relates to the question of how to best scale up implementation of instructional improvements. Coburn (2003) describes scale as more than the quantification of teachers who are implementing reform practices. Instead, scale involves deep change, "change that goes beyond surface structures or procedures (such as change in materials, classroom organization, or the addition of specific activities) to alter teachers' beliefs, norms of social interaction, and pedagogical principles as enacted in the curriculum" (p. 4). Such efforts at deep change are thought to result in more comprehensive, expansive, genuine, and lasting reforms. Thus understood, measures of scale should aim to capture the spirit of the reform and not mere compliance. Moreover, this conceptualization of scale seems to belie the idea of mandating compliance with instructional reform policies and interaction with instructional teacher leaders.

On the other hand, research on policy implementation also suggests that changing teacher beliefs about teaching and learning may first require a change in practice. Such a theory of action reflects the view that "beliefs follow action" and seems to suggest a need to mandate changes in practices in an effort to prompt deep change. Lord et al. (2008) raise this issue with regard to instructional teacher leadership. They question whether teacher leaders will be able to bring instructional reforms to scale if they work with small numbers of willing teachers and provide gentle feedback rather than promoting widespread critical reflection and critique. Teachers have historically shied away from these professional norms of dialogue and deprivatized practice (Lortie, 1975). Thus, moving teacher leaders from more cautious "show-and-tell" strategies to active engagement in difficult conversations may not happen without a combination of supportive capacity building and mandated reform.

Should teacher leaders take on a role in the formal evaluation of teachers? Would it lead to increased influence of instructional teacher leaders on a larger number of teachers' practice and thus begin to address the challenge of scale? Or must change in practice precede beliefs about teaching and learning? What are the tradeoffs between scale and developing relationships of trust with teachers?

Secondary-Level Teacher Leaders

This volume focuses specifically on elementary-level teacher leader roles and does not include case studies of instructional teacher leaders working in secondary school settings. There were three reasons we did not include secondary cases in this volume: (a) schools and districts have been slow to adopt formal roles for secondary-level instructional teacher leaders; (b) there is little research on secondary-level instructional teacher leadership; and (c) the authors' research and scholarship has focused on elementary roles.

To date, most of the growth in instructional teacher leader roles has occurred primarily at the elementary level, as evident in comprehensive reform models and the federal Reading First initiative, both of which have focused their improvement efforts on elementary schools. Yet a recent push for secondary reform has prompted some districts to investigate the possibility of implementing instructional teacher leader roles at the middle and secondary levels (Mangin, 2008a). There are examples of secondary-level instructional coaches being implemented on a large scale in urban areas, like Chicago's Instructional Delivery System (IDS) initiative being funded by the Bill and Melinda Gates Foundation, in which approximately 65 high school coaches are mentoring teachers in English, math, and science in 40 high schools (B. Feranchak, personal communication, April 2009). In support of these kinds of initiatives, the International Reading Association has developed standards for secondary-level literacy coaches.

Nevertheless, secondary-level teacher leader initiatives are moving more slowly than those in elementary schools, perhaps due to concerns about potential organizational obstacles that may inhibit the success of teacher leader initiatives at the secondary level. This concern appears to be justified. Supovitz (2008) found that instructional teacher leadership in high schools is enacted informally and situationally; that a variety of leaders emerge at the high school level based on the issues teachers face in their work rather than in relation to a formal teacher leader position. A study of middle schools found that teachers' preoccupation with subject area mastery inhibited them from seeking assistance from a literacy coach (Smith, 2006). These findings imply that organizational and institutional differences between elementary and secondary schools may lead to fundamental differences in the enactment of teacher leader roles in these settings.

Moreover, the absence of a robust body of research on secondary-level instructional teacher leadership makes it difficult to interpret secondary-level case studies in relationship to empirical evidence. One of our goals in writing this volume was to draw and build upon the emergent research on instructional teacher leaders to create research-based resources that would, in turn, contribute to that developing research. Thus, existing research was used to shape the case studies and helped to define the interpretive lenses we applied in the teaching notes. Our commitment to this research-based approach contributed to our decision to not include cases focused on secondary-level instructional teacher leaders.

Finally, given that instructional teacher leader roles have developed primarily in elementary schools, our research and scholarship have focused on that schooling level. Had we opted to write secondary-level case studies, they would not have been based on real cases. Again, we felt that the use of real cases, from schools in which we collected data over a number of years, was a critical component of the volume and an essential strength.

The question remains, what lessons learned from the elementary-level cases in this volume can be applied to instances of secondary-level teacher leadership? The way this volume has conceptualized role functions of instructional teacher leaders at the elementary level may be largely parallel in high schools. A brief analysis of the role functions of IDS coaches in Chicago revealed that coaches undertook content presentations, classroom visits, study groups, co-planning, demonstration lessons, and co-teaching (Michael Lach, personal communication, March 2009). Many of the themes highlighted in this book—time management, relationships with teachers, work with other leaders, teacher leader skills, work with the principal, and school norms and structures—may be applicable to the work of secondary-level teacher leaders. This remains an area in need of further investigation.

The Role of Content

In our previous book, we discussed a set of research topics related to instructional teacher leadership that merit additional inquiry. One topic of prominence was how the instructional content area may influence the work of instructional teacher leaders. In particular, we noted: "What remains unexplored is the relationship between subject area, content expertise, and effective instructional teacher leadership. Does teacher leadership in the areas of math or science, as studied by Manno and Firestone, require a different type of content knowledge than teacher leadership in literacy or another subject area?" (quoted in Mangin & Stoelinga, 2008, p. 188). As we write our closing thoughts in this volume, this need remains.

Similar to our thoughts on secondary- versus elementary-level instructional teacher leadership, we believe that the case studies included in this volume, regardless of whether they are examples of math or literacy teacher leaders, contain topics and lessons that are universally applicable regardless of subject matter. For example, building relationships with the principal and teachers is likely to be critical to the success of an instructional teacher leader, regardless of whether she or he is supporting teachers in literacy, mathematics, or another subject area. Similarly, school culture and norms have an effect on the efforts of a teacher leader in any subject.

That said, it is impossible to know the extent to which the subject matter differentially influences the work of instructional teacher leaders. Are teachers more open to external expertise from a math coach than they would be from a literacy coach? Would mandated interaction with a literacy coach be more palatable than with a math coach? Does one subject area lend itself to deprivatized practice and shared dialogue more than another subject area? Might the effectiveness of different coaching functions vary with the subject matter?

DEFINING AN OPTIMISTIC PATH

The questions we have raised are challenging. They engage the fundamental question of whether instructional teacher leadership "works" and under what conditions. The quest to find the answers is certainly daunting. We close this inquiry, however, with a tone of optimism. It is an optimism that permeates much of our observations of and conversations with the instructional teacher leaders who so generously shared their time, lives, perspectives, and voices with us. "I do this work because I believe all teachers can teach, just as a good teacher believes all students can learn," one of the teacher leaders stated. "I am eternally optimistic that my work can improve teaching and learning in this school," stated another. Despite the daunting challenges that we have described in this volume, there is a sense of hope and commitment among teacher leaders about the importance, influence, and potential for school improvement that results from their work. It is with this sense of optimism that we move forward: as teacher leaders engaged in the work of improving instruction; as principals and district staff striving to improve schools; and as scholars preoccupied by debates about the best form and functions of teacher leader work.

Appendix

Table 1.1. Key Role Functions in Vignettes 1–3 (Vignettes, Activity 1)

Role Function	*Susan*	*Matt*	*Stella*
Resource Management			
Demonstration Lesson			
Presentation			
Study Group			
Co-Plan			
Co-Teach			
Preconferencing			
Debriefing Conference			
Grade-Level Meeting			
Peer Coaching			
Observation			

Table 1.2. Key Role Functions for Instructional Teacher Leaders (ITL)
(Vignettes, Activity 1)

Role Function	Definition
Resource Management	The ITL works with teachers to identify, locate, and provide appropriate instructional resources.
Demonstration Lesson	The ITL demonstrates a particular instructional strategy, method, practice, or use of materials. Such a demonstration may be a "model lesson," or it may represent a learning opportunity for both the ITL and the classroom teacher.
Presentation	The ITL facilitates teachers' learning in an out-of-classroom learning activity. This may include training at a faculty meeting, in-service day, or workshop-style session.
Study Group	The ITL works with a subset of teachers to investigate and study an instructional topic or challenge. This may include a Japanese-style "lesson study," collaborative analysis of student performance, book study, etc.
Co-Plan	The ITL works with a teacher or group of teachers to plan instructional lessons. This may include aligning instructional content across teachers, grade levels, or with curriculum standards; planning which instructional strategies to use to meet students' needs; discussing how to organize and execute a lesson; or discussing the content knowledge necessary to guide and promote student learning.
Co-Teach	The ITL assists the classroom teacher in the execution of a lesson.
Preconferencing	The ITL engages in a discussion with the classroom teacher prior to demonstrating or observing in the classroom. The conversation focuses on goals for the demonstration/observation, particular instructional strategies or practices to focus on, and the student learning anticipated.
Debriefing Conference	The ITL discusses with the classroom teacher following a demonstration lesson or classroom observation. The conversation focuses on what each person observed related to teaching and learning, areas of insight, areas for growth, and next steps for teacher learning and instructional improvement.
Grade-Level Meeting	The ITL works with teachers in a grade level to improve teaching and learning through analysis of student performance data and teachers' instructional practices. The focus is on improving teaching and learning through systematic analysis, discussion, and modification of instruction.
Peer Coaching	The ITL engages in a conversation with an individual teacher about concerns related to student performance and instructional practice.
Observation	The ITL observes teaching and learning in the classroom for the purpose of assessing needs and practices and identifying areas of strength and areas for improvement.

Table 1.3. Susan's Schedule (Vignettes, Activity 2)

Time Period	Monday	Tuesday	Wednesday	Thursday	Friday
8:30–9:00	Prepare materials for tomorrow's demo with 4th-grade teachers:	Ms. Bell, 4th: Model "Eating Fractions" by Bruce McMillan during literacy block	Prepare materials for tomorrow's demo with 3rd-grade teachers:	Ms. Smith, 3rd: Model "One Hundred Hungry Ants" by Elinor Pinczes during literacy block.	Plan for Monday's staff meeting: probability activities. • Supplies • Worksheets • Sign-up sheet
9:00–9:30	• Get copies of book on fractions: *The 25 Mixtec Cats* by Mathew Golub.	Mrs. Flint, 4th: Model "Eating Fractions" by Bruce McMillan during literacy block	• Get copies of book on multiplication: *Each Orange Had Eight Slices* by Paul Giganti.	Mrs. Tupper, 3rd: Model "One Hundred Hungry Ants" by Elinor Pinczes during literacy block.	
9:30–10:00	• Prepare handout on how to incorporate math into literacy.	Ms. Davis, 4th: Model "Eating Fractions" by Bruce McMillan during literacy block	• Prepare handout on how to incorporate math into literacy.	Ms. Jenkins, 3rd: Model "One Hundred Hungry Ants" by Elinor Pinczes during literacy block.	
10:00–10:30	Prepare 1st-grade pentasquares lesson.	Debrief with Mrs. Flint when kids are at Art.	Prepare 2nd-grade pentasquares lesson.	Follow-up with Mrs. Bartlet. Did she try activities? Next steps?	Prepare materials for 5th-grade teachers.
10:30–11:00		Prepare kindergarten pentasquares lesson.			

(continued)

Table 1.3. (continued)

Lunch		Debrief with Ms. Bell.		Debrief with Ms Smith.	
12:30–1:30	Mrs. Bartlet, 1st: Model pentasquares lesson. Leave materials.	Ms. Small, kindergarten: Model pentasquares lesson. Leave materials.	Mr. Martin, 2nd: Model pentasquares lesson. Leave materials.	Mr. Clark, 1st: Model pentasquares lesson. Leave materials.	Mrs. Keller, 2nd: Model pentasquares lesson. Leave materials.
1:30–2:00	Follow-up Mr. Martin re: last week's demo. Did he try activities? Next steps?	Follow-up Mr. Clark re: Last week's demo. Did he try activities? Next steps? Confirm Thur.	Follow-up Mrs. Keller re: Last week's demo. Did she try activities? Next steps? Confirm Fri.	Attend 5th-grade team meeting.	Preplan probability activities for each grade level. Anticipate all grades.
2:00–2:30	Review last year's scores on probability questions. Examine lessons in math texts.	Browse online for probability activities and resources.	Plan next month's family math night. Answer e-mail.	Debrief with Mrs. Tupper during gym.	
2:30–3:00					
3:00–3:30	Talk with Ms. Capp about 5th-grade team mtg.	Debrief with Ms. Davis after school.		Debrief with Ms. Jenkins after school.	Brief principal on content for Monday.

Table 1.4. Stella's Schedule (Vignettes, Activity 2)

Time Period	Monday	Tuesday	Wednesday	Thursday	Friday
8:30–9:00	Pre-observation meeting, Ms. Laramie, 2nd	Grade-level meeting, 3rd-grade teachers	Pre-demonstration meeting, Mr. Alphonso, 1st	Observation, Ms. Ortega, 3rd	Co-teaching with Ms. Garcia, 1st
9:00–9:30	Observation, Ms. Laramie, 2nd	Grade-level meeting, 1st-grade teachers	Guided reading demonstration, Mr. Alphonso, 1st		
9:30–10:00		Grade level meeting, 2nd-grade teachers			
10:00–10:30	Meeting with IEP team	Grade-level meeting, kindergarten teachers	Pre-observation meeting, Ms. Ortega, 3rd	Observation, Ms. Smith, 3rd	Prepare for next week's staff development presentation
10:30–11:00	Review and update student IEPs	Assist with 8-week assessment in Ms. Carver's room, 3rd	Pre-observation meeting, Ms. Smith, 3rd		
Lunch	Post-observation debriefing, Ms. Laramie, 2nd	Assist with 8-week assessment in Ms. Oberlin's room, 2nd	Post-demonstration debriefing, Mr. Alphonso, 1st	Post-observation debriefing, Ms. Ortega, 3rd	Post-co-teaching debriefing with Ms. Garcia, 1st

(continued)

Table 1.4. (continued)

12:30–1:30	Plan SFA parent event: • Prepare materials • Make invites • Contact parent leaders • Order food	Prepare demonstration lesson for Mr. Alphonso, 1st	Assist with 8-week assessment in Mr. Alphonso's room	Work on updating IEPs with school counselor	Pick up completed 8-week assessments
1:30–2:00			Prepare for next week's staff development presentation	Prepare co-teaching lesson with Ms. Garcia, 1st	Enter 8-week assessment data into system; analyze data
2:00–2:30	Weekly meeting with principal	Conference call with SFA national office about progress in implementation		Pick up completed 8-week assessments	
2:30–3:00	Weekly meeting with bilingual coordinator		Answer e-mail	Distribute materials to teachers	
3:00–3:30	Distribute 8-week assessment materials to teachers	Answer e-mail	Phone call with neighboring SFA school literacy facilitator about implementation challenges	Post-observation debriefing, Ms. Smith, 3rd	Create new student groups based on 8-week assessment

Figure 1.1. Teacher Leader Job Description (Vignettes, Activity 4)

JOB DESCRIPTION: MATH LEAD TEACHER

TITLE:	Education Program Specialist (Math Lead Teacher)
QUALIFICATIONS:	(1) A valid Elementary and/or Mathematics certificate
	(2) Knowledge of the state standards and NCTM standards
	(3) Additional coursework in Mathematics
	(4) Experience in providing professional development in Math
	(5) Required criminal history review background check and proof of U.S. citizenship or legal resident alien status
REPORTS TO:	Principal
	Supervisor of Curriculum and Instruction
RESPONSIBILITIES:	The Math Lead Teacher is responsible to provide assistance to faculty and instruction to students in an effort to bring all students to grade level or beyond in Math skills.

PERFORMANCE RESPONSIBILITIES:

(1) Provide demonstration lessons, co-teaching, coaching, and inservice to faculty to improve general math instruction.

(2) Review math materials/resources and make recommendations for inclusion in the math program.

(3) Promote school-wide programs/incentives to enhance interest in math.

(4) Provide parent programs involving basic skills parents and parents of targeted groups of students.

(5) Articulate math programs between the elementary, middle and high schools.

(6) Provide small group instruction to students in need of math remediation/enrichment on a limited basis.

(7) Other duties as deemed appropriate by the administration.

TERMS OF EMPLOYMENT:	Ten month position.
SALARY:	Salary as per negotiated agreement.
EVALUATION:	Performance of this job will be evaluated annually with provisions of the Board policy on Evaluation of Personnel.

Figure 1.2. Teacher Leader Job Description (Vignettes, Activity 4)

JOB DESCRIPTION: ELEMENTARY MATH SUPPORT TEACHER

The core business of schools in the School District is to develop knowledge work that will promote student engagement and authentic learning.

QUALIFICATIONS:

  Appropriate state teacher certificate
  Strong interpersonal and communication skills
  Ability to communicate with students, parents, school staff, and community
  Knowledge of field
  Knowledge of/or willingness to deliver instruction according to state curriculum standards
  Personal attributes that include love of children, flexibility, and sense of humor
  Required criminal history background check

REPORTS TO:

Principal/Curriculum Supervisor

JOB GOAL:

Elementary Math Support Teachers will support the implementation of the math program, Math Trailblazers. Support teachers will receive special training from the Kendall Hunt Company, learning how to work with teachers to promote best practices in the math classroom. The responsibilities of the job will include meeting with teachers to discuss the progress of implementation, to share instructional ideas, and to support classroom teachers. They also may take a part in the math study groups. Overall, these Support Teachers will play an important role in the staff development plan for district classroom teachers.

ROLES FOR MATH SUPPORT TEACHER:

  • Math resource person for staff and principals
  • Modeling lessons in classrooms
  • Playing a supporting role in classrooms
  • Planning/reflecting with grade level teams
  • Peer coaching
  • Collecting data
  • Supporting teachers with pacing
  • Informal classroom visitations
  • Looking ahead at upcoming units
  • Working with supervisors and other Math Support Teachers toward consistency
  • Communicating with principals
  • Being a liaison for district/federal grants
  • Providing informal and formal staff development
  • Keeping up with current math practice and research through reading, participating in listservs, attending conferences
  • Sharing effective best practices and strategies with teachers
  • Sharing ideas and data with staff
  • Connecting with other districts using standards based math
  • Act as a connecting link between staff and implementation of curriculum
  • Supporting parent connections (disseminating information/math night)
  • Performs other related duties as assigned

TERMS OF EMPLOYMENT:

Ten-month work year. Salary and work year to be determined by the Board.

EVALUATION:

Performance of this job will be evaluated in accordance with provisions of Board policies on Evaluation of Professional Personnel.

Figure 1.3. Teacher Leader Job Description (Vignettes, Activity 4)

JOB DESCRIPTION: ELEMENTARY READING COACH

This employee is responsible for planning and coordinating the primary and intermediate reading and language arts program at the school level.

Duties of this position include but are not limited to:

1. Staff Development:
   a. Participating in staff development sessions conducted by the district.
   b. Providing staff development for teachers, volunteers, parents, paraprofessionals, administrators, and other appropriate personnel as needed.
2. Instructional Program:
   a. Coordinating the school reading and language arts and primary programs both horizontally and vertically.
   b. Assisting classroom teachers in planning reading/language arts programs and primary and intermediate programs.
   c. Assisting all teachers with teaching/learning strategies that promote comprehension in all subject areas.
   d. Modeling reading and language arts instruction in primary and intermediate classrooms.
   e. Coordinating the developmental aspects of the primary and intermediate programs.
   f. Collaboratively selecting and coordinating (with the approval of the principal) all reading and language arts materials used in the classrooms.
   g. Coordinating in identified schools activities of the Chapter I reading program and or the Migrant program so as to insure continuity between the regular program and federal programs.
   h. Assisting in assuring continuity between regular programs and other special areas (e.g., ESOL, ESE, Pre-K).
   i. Assisting teachers with instructional interventions.
   j. Assisting with the staffings of students for specific services (e.g., ESOL, ESE).
   k. Implementing in the school the School Board curriculum outcomes associated with reading and language arts.
   l. Maintaining current and efficient records including the preparation of reports.
3. Evaluation:
   a. Implementing the county portfolio system.
   b. Assisting teachers in assessing students for appropriate instruction.
   c. Evaluating students with severe problems that may require additional support services.
   d. Submitting appropriate data and reports.
4. Public Relations:
   a. Interpreting the school's reading/learning program for staff, parents, and members of the community.
   b. Serving as part of the County-wide committee in developing activities and programs to disseminate information.
5. Other Responsibilities:
   Serving as part of a county-wide team to provide assistance and promote cooperation among schools.

REQUIRED QUALIFICATIONS:

1. Master's degree or within 6 hours of earning a Master's degree.
2. Current enrollment in a program leading to certification in reading. The expectation is that the applicant will complete the program.
3. Three years of teaching experience.
4. Experience with elementary programs.

DESIRED QUALIFICATIONS:

1. Master's degree in reading.
2. Experience with integrated curriculum.
3. Gesell examiner training.
4. Experience in providing staff development for adults.
5. Experience in a like position.

Table 2.1. Establishing the Facts of the Case (Open-Ended Cases 1–5)

	Establishing the Facts of the Case
What is known about the teacher leader's professional background?	
What is known about the teacher leader's role?	
What is known about the school/district where the teacher leader works?	
What is known about the teacher leader's colleagues & supervisors?	
Other potentially relevant facts related to the case:	
What potentially relevant information is NOT known about the case and what reasonable assumptions might be made?	

Table 2.2. Charting Erin's Tasks (Open-Ended Case 1, Step 3, Part 1)

Teacher Leader Task	Target Population	Purpose/Rationale	Frequency	Measure of Success

Table 2.3. Dialogue Between Erin and Mrs. Thompson (Open-Ended Case 1, Step 3, Part 2)

DIALOGUE	ANALYTIC COMMENTARY
	This exchange demonstrates . . .
Erin:	
Mrs. Thompson:	

Table 2.4. Analyzing the Literacy Coach Role at Jefferson Elementary (Open-Ended Case 2, Step 2, Part 3)

Obstacle to Leadership	Did obstacle exist? (Y or N)	Strategy in Case	Improved Strategy
Lack of role definition			
Lack of administrator support			
Isolation of classroom teachers			
Norms of teaching: Autonomy			
Norms of teaching: Egalitarianism			
Norms of teaching: Seniority			

Table 2.5. Micropolitics at Maribel Elementary (Open-Ended Case 3, Step 2, Part 1)

Factions or Actors	Characteristics or Interests	Evidence

Table 2.6. Eight Principal Support Strategies (Open-Ended Case 4, Step 2, Part 4)

Principal Support Strategies	Extent of Strategy	Evidence/Notes
Collaboratively build and monitor an action plan		
Negotiate the relationship		
Be available		
Provide access to human and fiscal resources		
Maintain the focus on instructional leadership		
Help maintain balance to avoid overload		
Protect relationship with peers		
Provide leadership development opportunities		

Table 2.7. Eight Steps to Improve Data Usage at Blackstone (Open-Ended Case 5, Step 2, Part 1)

"Data Wise" Steps	Resources	Strengths	Weaknesses
Organize for Collaborative Work			
Build Assessment Literacy			
Create Data Overview			
Dig into Student Data			
Examine Instruction			
Develop Action Plan			
Plan to Assess Progress			
Act and Assess			

Table 3.1. Barley School: Establishing the Facts of the Case

	Establishing the Facts of the Case
What is known about the reforms taking place at Barley School?	
What is known about the principal of Barley School?	
What is known about the teachers who work at Barley School?	
What is known about the literacy facilitator?	
Other potentially relevant facts related to the case:	
What potentially relevant information is NOT known about the case and what reasonable assumptions might be made?	

Table 3.2. Barley School: Why Reforms Fail (Application to Case)

1. FAULTY MAPS OF CHANGE
2. COMPLEX PROBLEMS
3. SYMBOLS OVER SUBSTANCE
4. IMPATIENT AND SUPERFICIAL SOLUTIONS
5. MISUNDERSTANDING RESISTANCE
6. ATTRITION OF POCKETS OF SUCCESS
7. MISUSE OF KNOWLEDGE ABOUT THE CHANGE PROCESS

Table 3.3. Barley School: Propositions for Success (Application to Case)

1. CHANGE IS LEARNING—LOADED WITH UNCERTAINTY
2. CHANGE IS A JOURNEY, NOT A BLUEPRINT
3. PROBLEMS ARE OUR FRIENDS
4. CHANGE IS RESOURCE-HUNGRY
5. CHANGE REQUIRES THE POWER TO MANAGE IT
6. CHANGE IS SYSTEMIC
7. ALL LARGE-SCALE CHANGE IS IMPLEMENTED LOCALLY

Table 3.4. Sexton School District: Establishing the Facts of the Case

	Establishing the Facts of the Case
What is known about the reforms taking place in Sexton School District?	
What is known about the superintendent of Sexton School District?	
What is known about the math coach at Carver Elementary?	
What is known about opportunities for professional growth in Sexton School District?	
Other potentially relevant facts related to the case:	
What potentially relevant information is NOT known about the case and what reasonable assumptions might be made?	

Table 3.5. Aurora School: Establishing the Facts of the Case

	Establishing the Facts of the Case
What is known about the reforms taking place at Aurora School?	
What is known about the principal of Aurora School?	
What is known about the teachers who work at Aurora School?	
What is known about the literacy coach?	
Other potentially relevant facts related to the case:	
What potentially relevant information is NOT known about the case and what reasonable assumptions might be made?	

References

Allen, J. (2006). *Becoming a literacy leader: Supporting learning and change*. Portland, ME: Stenhouse.

Ball, S. (1987). *The micro-politics of the school: Towards a theory of school organization*. London: Methuen.

Berman, P., & McLaughlin, M. (1977). *Federal programs supporting educational change, VII: Factors affecting implementation and continuation*. Santa Monica, CA: Rand.

Blase, J. (1991). (Ed.). *The politics of life in schools: Power, conflict and cooperation* (pp. 120–130). Newbury Park, CA: Sage.

Blase, J. (1993). The micropolitics of effective school-based leadership: Teachers' perspectives. *Educational Administration Quarterly, 29*(20), 142–163.

Blase, J., & Blase, J. (1998). *Handbook of instructional leadership: How really good principals promote teaching and learning*. Thousand Oaks, CA: Corwin Press.

Boudett, K. P., City, E. A., & Murnane, R. J. (2006). The "Data Wise" improvement process: Eight steps for using test data to improve teaching and learning. *Harvard Education Letter, 22*(1), 1–3.

Bridges, E. M. (1992). *Problem-based learning for administrators*. Eugene, OR: ERIC Clearinghouse on Educational Management.

Bridges, E. M., & Hallinger, P. (1992). *Problem-based learning for administrators*: ERIC Clearinghouse on Educational Management, University of Oregon.

Bryk, A., Camburn, E., & Louis, K. S. (1999). Professional community in Chicago elementary schools: Facilitating factors and organizational consequences. *Educational Administration Quarterly, 35*(Supplement), 751–781.

Bryk, A. S., & Schneider, B. (2002). *Trust in schools: A core resource for improvement*. New York: Russell Sage Foundation.

Bryk, A., Sebring, P., Kerbow, D., Rollow, S., & Easton, J. (1998). *Charting Chicago school reform*. Boulder, CO: Westview Press.

Burns, M., Felux, C., & Snowdy, P. (2006). *The math coach field guide: Charting your course*. Sausalito, CA: Math Solutions.

Camburn, E. M., Kimball, S. M., & Lowenhaupt, R. (2008). Going to scale with teacher leadership: Lessons learned from a districtwide literacy coach initiative. In M. M. Mangin & S. R. Stoelinga (Eds.), *Effective teacher leadership: Using research to inform and reform* (pp. 120–143). New York: Teachers College Press.

Chubb, J. E., & Moe, T. M. (1990). *Politics, markets and America's schools*. Washington, DC: Brookings Institution.

Coburn, C. E. (2003). Rethinking scale: Moving beyond numbers to deep and lasting change. *Educational Researcher, 32*(6), 3–12.

Cohen, D. K., & Hill, H. C. (2001). *Learning policy: When state education reform works*. New Haven, CT: Yale University Press.

Copland, M. (2003). Leadership of inquiry: Building and sustaining capacity for school improvement. *Educational Evaluation and Policy Analysis, 25*, 375–395.

Datnow, A., & Castellano, M. E. (2001). Managing and guiding school reform: Leadership in Success For All schools. *Educational Administration Quarterly, 37*(2), 219–249.

Davidson, J. (2003). A new role in facilitating school reform: The case of the Educational Technologist. *Teachers College Record, 105*(5), 729–752.

Drago-Severson, E. (2004). *Helping teachers learn: Principals' leadership for adult growth and development*. Thousand Oaks, CA: Corwin Press.

Drago-Severson, E. (2006). How can you better support teachers' growth? *The Learning Principal, 1*(6), pp. 1, 6–7.

Drago-Severson, E. (2008). *Leading adult learning: Promising practices for supporting adult growth and development*. Thousand Oaks, CA: Corwin Press.

Drago-Severson, E., & Pinto, K. (2004). From barriers to breakthroughs: Principals' strategies for overcoming challenges to teachers' transformational learning. *The Journal of School Leadership, 14*, 653–685.

Elmore, R., & Burney, D. (1999). *Investing in teacher learning*. In L. Darling-Hammond and G. Sykes (Eds.), *Teaching as a learning profession* (pp. 236–291). San Francisco: Jossey-Bass.

Firestone, W. A., Mangin, M. M., Martinez, M. C., & Polovsky, T. (2005). Content and coherence in district professional development: Three case studies. *Educational Administration Quarterly, 41*, 413–448.

Fuhrman, S. H. (1999). *Policy brief: Reporting on issues in education reform*. Philadelphia, PA: Consortium for Policy Research in Education.

Fullan, M. (2000a). The return of large-scale reform. *Journal of Educational Change, 1*, 1–23.

Fullan, M. (2000b). The three stories of education reform. *Phi Delta Kappan, 81*(8), 581–584.

Fullan, M., & Miles, M. B. (1990). Getting reform right: What works and what doesn't. *Phi Delta Kappa, 17*(10), 744–753.

Gabriel, J. G. (2005). *How to thrive as a teacher leader*. Alexandria, VA: Association for Supervision and Curriculum Development.

Garet, M. S., Porter, A. C., Desimone, L., Birman, B. F., & Yoon, K. S. (2001). What makes professional development effective? Results from a national sample of teachers. *American Educational Research Journal, 38*(4), 915–945.

Hall, L., & McKeen, R.L. (1989). Increased professionalism in the work environment of teachers through peer coaching. *Education, 109*(3), 310–316.

Halverson, R., Grigg, J., Prichett, R., & Thomas, C. (2005). *The new instructional leadership: Creating data-driven instructional systems in schools*. WCER Working Paper 2005–9, Wisconsin Center for Education Research, University of Wisconsin–Madison.

Halverson, R., & Thomas, C. N. (2008). Student services practices as a model for data-driven instructional leadership. In M. M. Mangin & S. R. Stoelinga (Eds.),

Effective teacher leadership: Using research to inform and reform (pp. 163–182). New York: Teachers College Press.

Hawley, W. D., & Valli, L. (1999). The essentials of effective professional development. In L. Darling-Hammond & G. Sykes (Eds.), *Teaching as the learning profession: Handbook of policy and practice* (pp. 127–150). San Francisco: Jossey-Bass.

Hightower, A. M., Knapp, M. S., Marsh, J., & McLaughlin, M. (2002). *School districts and instructional renewal.* New York: Teachers College Press.

Hill, P. T. (2006). *Put learning first: A portfolio approach to public schools.* Washington DC: Progressive Policy Institute.

Hill, P. T., Campbell, C., & Harvey, J. (2000). *It takes a city: Getting serious about urban school reform.* Washington, DC: Brookings Institution.

Iannaccone, I. (1991). Micropolitics of education: What and why. *Education and Urban Society, 23*(4), 465–471.

Iannaccone, L., & Lutz, F. W. (1994). The crucible of democracy: The local arena. *Journal of Education Policy, 9*(5), 39–52.

Ivory, G., & Gonzalez, M. L. (1999). The quandaries solved by case-based teaching. *The Journal of Cases in Educational Leadership, 2*(3), 1–8.

Johnson, S. M., & Donaldson, M. L. (2007). Overcoming the obstacles to leadership. *Educational Leadership, 65*(1), 8–13.

Katz, M. B., Fine, M., & Simon, E. (1997). Poking around: Outsiders view Chicago school reform. *Teachers College Record, 99*(1), 117–157.

King, K. P., & Lawler, P. A. (2003). Trends and issues in the professional development of teachers of adults. In K. P. King & P. A. Lawler (Eds.), *New perspectives on designing and implementing professional development of teachers of adults* (pp. 5–13). New directions for adult and continuing education, no. 98. San Francisco: Jossey-Bass.

Kramer, R. M., & Tyler, T. R. (Eds). (1996). *Trust in organizations.* Thousand Oaks, CA: Sage.

Krupp, J. (1987). Mentoring: A means by which teachers become staff developers. *Journal of Staff Development, 8*(1), 12–15.

Kruse, S., Louis, K., & Bryk, A. (1994). *Building professional community in schools.* Madison, WI: Center on Organization & Restructuring Schools.

Kruse, S. D., Louis, K. S., & Bryk, A. (1995). *Professionalism and community: Perspectives on reforming urban schools.* Thousand Oaks, CA: Corwin.

Lachat, M. A., & Smith, S. (2005). Practices that support data use in urban schools. *Journal of Education for Students Placed at Risk, 10*(3), 333–349.

Lieberman, A. (Ed.). (1988). *Building a professional culture in schools.* New York: Teachers College Press.

Lindle, J. C. (1999). What can the study of micropolitics contribute to the practice of leadership in reforming schools? *School Leadership and Management, 19*(2), 171–178.

Little, J. W. (1990). The "mentor" phenomenon and the social organization of teaching. *Review of Research in Education, 16,* 345–369.

Lord, B., Cress, K., & Miller, B. (2008). Teacher leadership in support of large-scale mathematics and science education reform. In M. M. Mangin & S. R. Stoelinga

(Eds.), *Effective teacher leadership: Using research to inform and reform* (pp. 55–76). New York: Teachers College Press.

Lortie, D. (1975). *Schoolteacher: A sociological study*. Chicago: University of Chicago Press.

Louis, K. S., & Kruse, S. D. (1995). *Professionalism and community: Perspectives on reforming urban schools*. Thousand Oaks, CA: Corwin Press.

Louis, K. S., & Marks, H. M. (1998). Does professional community affect the classroom? Teachers' work and student experiences in restructuring schools. *American Journal of Education, 106*(4), 532–575.

Louis, K. S., Marks, H. M., & Kruse, S. D. (1996). Teachers' professional community in restructuring schools. *American Educational Research Journal, 33*(4), 757–798.

Malen, B. (1994). The micropolitics of education: Mapping the multiple dimensions of power relations in school politics. *Journal of Education Policy, 9*(5), 39–52.

Mangin, M. M. (2005). Distributed leadership and the culture of schools: Teacher leaders' strategies for gaining access to classrooms. *Journal of School Leadership, 15*(4), 456–484.

Mangin, M. M. (2006). Teacher leadership and instructional improvement: Teachers' perspectives. In W. K. Hoy & C. Miskel (Eds.), *Contemporary issues in educational policy and school outcomes* (pp. 159–192). Greenwich, CT: Information Age Publishing.

Mangin, M. M. (2007). Facilitating elementary principals' support for instructional teacher leadership. *Educational Administration Quarterly, 43*(3), 319–357.

Mangin, M. M. (2008a). *District context and the development of instructional teacher leader initiatives*. Paper^spresented at the Annual Meeting of the American Educational Research Association, Division A, New York.

Mangin, M. M. (2008b). The influence of organizational design on instructional teacher leadership. In M. M. Mangin & S. R. Stoelinga (Eds.), *Effective teacher leadership: Using research to inform and reform*. New York: Teachers College Press.

Mangin, M. M., & Stoelinga, S. R. (Eds.). (2008). *Effective teacher leadership: Using research to inform and reform*. New York: Teachers College Press.

Manno, C. M., & Firestone, W. A. (2008). Content is the subject: How teacher leaders with different subject knowledge interact with teachers. In M. M. Mangin & S. R. Stoelinga (Eds.), *Effective teacher leadership: Using research to inform and reform* (pp. 36–54) New York: Teachers College Press.

Marks, H. M., & Printy, S. M. (2003). Principal leadership & school performance: An integration of transformational & instructional leadership. *Educational Administration Quarterly, 39*(3), 370–397.

Marshall, C., & Scribner, J. D. (1991). It's all political. *Education and Urban Society, 23*(4), 347–355.

Massell, D. (2000). *The district role in building capacity: Four Strategies* (CPRE Research Brief NO. RB-32). Philadelphia: Consortium for Policy Research in Education.

Mawhinney, H. B. (1999). Reappraisal: The problems and prospects of studying the micropolitics of leadership in reforming schools. *School Leadership and Management, 19*(2), 159–170.

McLaughlin, M., & Mitra, D. (2003). *The cycle of inquiry as the engine of school reform: Lessons from the Bay Area School Reform Collaborative.* Report, Center for Research on the Context of Teaching, Stanford University, Stanford, CA.

McLaughlin, M., & Talbert, J. (2001). *Professional communities and the work of high school teaching.* Chicago: University of Chicago Press.

Moller, G., & Pankake, A. (2006). *Lead with me: A principal's guide to teacher leadership.* Larchmont, NY: Eye on Education.

Murphy, J. (2005). *Connecting teacher leadership and school improvement.* Thousand Oaks, CA: Corwin Press.

Murphy, J., Beck, L., Crawford, M., Hodges, A., & McGaughy, C. (2001). *The productive high school: Creating personalized academic communities.* Thousand Oaks, CA: Corwin Press.

Newmann, F., & Wehlage, G. (1995). *Successful school restructuring.* Madison, WI: Center on Organization and Restructuring of Schools.

Newmann, F. M., Smith, B., Allensworth, E., & Bryk, A. S. (2001). Instructional program coherence: What it is & why it should guide school improvement policy. *Educational Evaluation and Policy Analysis, 23*(4), 297–321.

Pankake, A., & Moller, G. (2007). What the teacher leader needs from the principal. *Journal of Staff Development, 28*(1), 32–36.

Payne, C. M. (2008). *So much reform, so little change: The persistence of failure in urban schools.* Cambridge, MA: Harvard University Press.

Popham, W. J., Cruse, K. L., Rankin, S. C., Sandifer, P. D., & Williams, P. L. (1985). Measurement-driven instruction: It's on the road. *Phi Delta Kappan, 66,* 628–634.

Printy, S. M. (2008). Leadership for teacher learning: A community of practice perspective. *Educational Administration Quarterly, 44*(2), 187–226.

Raywid, M. A. (1995). Professional community and its yield at Metro Academy. In K. S. Louis & S. D. Kruse (Eds.), *Professionalism and community: Perspectives on reforming urban schools* (pp. 45–75). Thousand Oaks, CA: Corwin Press.

Richardson, V., & Placier, P. (2001). Teacher change. In V. Richardson (Ed.), *Handbook of research on teaching* (4th ed., pp. 905–947). New York: Macmillan.

Rowan, B. (1990). Commitment and control: Alternative strategies for the organizational design of schools. *Review of Research in Education, 16,* 353–389.

Sabatier, P., & Mazmanian, D. (1979). The conditions of effective implementation: A guide to accomplishing policy objectives. *Policy Analysis, 5*(5), 481–504.

Schmoker, M. (2003). *First things first:* Demystifying data analysis. *Educational Leadership, 60*(5), 22–24.

Smith, A. T. (2006). *The middle school literacy coach: Roles, contexts, and connections to teaching.* Unpublished doctoral dissertation, University of Washington.

Smylie, M. A. (1997). Research on teacher leadership: Assessing the state of the art. In B. J. Biddle, T. L. Good, & I. F. Goodson (Eds.), *International handbook of teachers and teaching* (pp. 521–592). Boston: Kluwer Academic Publishers.

Smylie, M.A. (2008). Foreword. In M. M. Mangin & S. R. Stoelinga (Eds.), *Effective teacher leadership: Using research to inform and reform* (pp. ix–x). New York: Teachers College Press.

Smylie, M. A., & Brownlee-Conyers, J. (1992). Teacher leaders and their principals: Exploring the development of new working relationships. *Educational Administration Quarterly, 28*(2), 150–184.

Smylie, M. A., Conley, S., & Marks, H. M. (2002). Exploring new approaches to teacher leadership for school improvement. In J. Murphy (Ed.), *The educational leadership challenge: Redefining leadership for the 21st century: 101st yearbook of the National Society for the Study of Education* (Vol. 101, part 1, pp. 162–188). Chicago: University of Chicago Press.

Stein, M. K. (1998). *High performance learning communities in District 2: Report on year one implementation of school learning communities.* Pittsburgh, PA: University of Pittsburgh, Learning Research and Development Center. (Document Number ED429263.)

Stoelinga, S. R. (2006). *Seeking the "S" in CMSI: History and implementation of the science initiative.* Chicago: The PRAIRIE Group.

Stoelinga, S. R. (2008). Leading from above and below: Formal and informal teacher leadership. In M. M. Mangin & S. R. Stoelinga (Eds.), *Effective teacher leadership: Using research to inform and reform.* New York: Teachers College Press.

Stone, R., & Cuper, P. H. (2006). *Best practices for teacher leadership: What award-winning teachers do for their professional learning communities.* Thousand Oaks, CA: Corwin Press.

Supovitz, J. A. (2008). Instructional influence in American high schools. In M. M. Mangin & S. R. Stoelinga (Eds.), *Effective teacher leadership: Using research to inform and reform* (pp. 144–162). New York: Teachers College Press.

Sweeney, D. (2003). *Learning along the way: Professional development by and for teachers.* Portland, ME: Stenhouse.

Taylor, D. L., & Bogotch, I. E. (1994). School-level effects of teachers' participation in decision making. *Educational Evaluation and Policy Analysis, 16*(3), 302–319.

Taylor, J. E. (2008). Instructional coaching: The state of the art. In M. M. Mangin & S. R. Stoelinga (Eds.), *Effective teacher leadership: Using research to inform and reform* (pp. 10–35). New York: Teachers College Press.

Toll, C. A. (2005). *The literacy coach's survival guide: Essential questions and practical answers.* Newark, DE: International Reading Association.

Tschannen-Moran, M. (2009). Fostering teacher professionalism in schools: The role of leadership orientation and trust. *Educational Administration Quarterly, 45*(2), 217–247.

West, M. (1999). Micropolitics, leadership and all that . . . The need to increase the micropolitical awareness and skills of school leaders. *School Leadership and Management, 19*(2), 159–170.

York-Barr, J., & Duke, K. (2004). What do we know about teacher leadership? Findings from two decades of scholarship. *Review of Educational Research, 74*(3), 255–316.

York-Barr, J., Sommerness, J., & Hur, J. (2008). Teacher leadership. In T. L. Good (Ed.), *21st century education: A reference handbook* (pp. 12–20). Thousand Oaks, CA: Sage Publications.

Young, V. M. (2006). Teachers' use of data: Loose coupling, agenda setting, and team norms. *American Journal of Education, 112,* 521–548.

Index

About the Authors

Sara Ray Stoelinga is a senior research analyst at the Consortium on Chicago School Research at the University of Chicago. She received her Ph.D. in sociology from the University of Chicago. She previously worked as an assistant research professor at the University of Illinois–Chicago conducting education evaluation in the Chicago Public Schools. Her research focuses on teacher and principal leadership in school reform efforts, the sociology of education, and organizational change in schools. Her recent publications include *Effective Teacher Leadership: Using Research to Inform and Reform*, a book published by Teachers College Press that she co-edited with Melinda M. Mangin.

Melinda M. Mangin is an assistant professor in educational administration at Michigan State University. She received her Ph.D. from Rutgers University, where she conducted research at the Center for Educational Policy Analysis. Mangin's career in education began as a public high school Spanish teacher in New York City. Presently, her research focuses on the contexts that influence teacher leadership and instructional improvement. Her recent publications include *Effective Teacher Leadership: Using Research to Inform and Reform*, a book published by Teachers College Press that she co-edited with Sara Ray Stoelinga.